The 42ⁿᵈ Generation
Sons of Jesus

By
Dr. S. Kiwi Kalloo

Copyright © 2013 by Kiwi S. Kalloo
All rights reserved

All rights reserved under International copyright law. Contents and / or cover may not be reproduced in whole or in part in any form without the express written consent of the author.

Printed in the United States of America

International Standard Book Number:
978-1-888081-87-9

Published and formatted by

GOOD NEWS FELLOWSHIP MINISTRIES
220 Sleepy Creek Rd.
Macon, GA 31210
Phone: (478) 757-8071

Vision

To establish people in the Heart of God
in the Principles of the Kingdom in Worship, Sonship and Maturity.

Mission & Purpose

To teach people to know the heart of God and to become mature Christians; to provide resources to the body of Christ that would minister to the nations of the world by sharing the love of Christ through the preaching and teaching of the Word of God.

Using the tools and resources, through a paradigm of kingdom concepts, to cause the hearts of men and women embrace the message of the cross, to become hungry and thirsty for the heart of God; culturizing the nations with the mind of Christ.

Dedication

To the Maker of all and the reason that I exist, the one true and living God, the sweetest most awesome, exciting person that I know—the Holy Spirit.

To my loving wife, Lisa, who is the source of encouragement and inspiration for my life.

To my children Joanna, Justin, and Jessica. The blessings which God have made real to me.

To my Mom and Dad for being instrumental in me becoming the man that I am today.

Acknowledgements

First, I would like to appreciate the love of my life, my beautiful wife and my best friend, Lisa, for the will to move on, and the spirit to accomplish. She is my driving force to success.

To my children, Joanna, Justin and Jessica, for being my joy and pride.

To my parents, Benjamin and Zulaika, for gracing me with birth, thus, allowing me freedom to become the man that I am today.

To my faithful Pastor and friend, Dr. David C. Yankana, to whom I have submitted as leader and bishop of my soul. He is truly a man of the Word and a man of honor.

To my faithful Pastor and friend, Pastor Pepe R. Ramnath, who has been there for my family and me through some of the most crucial times of our lives. His vision, purpose, character, integrity as an exemplary Father figure is what was displayed before us, which taught me to walk softly before God and to prepare an atmosphere for His presence. He is the Senior Pastor of the Miramar Kingdom Community Center formerly Miramar Christian Center Church located in Miramar Florida.

All my friends and fellow workers in Christ Jesus and the many Fathers that have played influential and roles in helping to form and shape the Christ in me.

Pastor Joseph Lamothe, His Eminence Most Reverend Dr. Madhu Krishan, Apostle Steve Everett, Apostle Thamo Naidoo, Apostle Yasser Rivas, Dr. Richard Pinder, Dr. Apostle Sagie Y. Govender, and Pastor Cathy Walker.

I would like to acknowledge Deyon Singh for his handiwork and creativity in being one of the greatest designers planet Earth could have ever been graced with. He is a very brilliant young man with a bright future ahead.

I would like to take this opportunity to acknowledge Jared Jacob for his diligence and patriotism regarding the Kingdom of God. Also, his unfailing efforts to getting this book edited and formatted to the publisher.

Endorsements

These are intriguing times in the Church of Jesus Christ. A new, mature generation of passionate believers are emerging from within its ranks. This generation is moved by the conviction to restore the apostolic tradition of Scripture to its culture, structures and function in creation. "The 42nd Generation" is a harbinger detailing the emergence of this mature company of people who seek to accurately represent Christ in the earth. Kiwi is an astute scholar of the Holy Scriptures skillfully extracting the mystery of Christ from the latter and number of Scripture. However, the brilliance of his skill is found in the application of these profound eschatological truths to the prophetic destiny of the Church. This book is a must read for those sons of God who desire to pursue deeper dimensions in their walk with God

Apostle Thamo Naidoo
GATE Ministries Sandton
www.thamonaidoo.com

The greatest sign and wonder witnessed in the earth today, is the manifestation of Christ in His Body. Christ is not only Jesus, who is the Head of the Church, seated at the right hand of the Father, but Christ (The Anointed One and His anointing) is also in His Body! We – His Body – are seated with Him in heavenly places. He is operating through His Body on the earth. There will be a generation on the earth that is first in time, first in rank and first in place; a pioneering company who must become "His Generation." This is the first fruit company who becomes the shoulders of Christ, the ones who display His Government on the earth as it is in Heaven. The Body must rule under the leadership of Christ. His desire is to lay His Head on His Body. (Matt 8:20) Every foreign governmental system must be eradicated from the Church, until His Body becomes the landing place of Christ.

I therefore congratulate Dr. Kalloo with his excellent work on clarifying this position of the Body of Christ, as the 42nd generation – the chosen generation. Christ is the progenitor of this generation, and we are of the same stock! As He is, so are we in this world. There must be a generation who will arise in the power and demonstration of His Word, and willing to declare these truths to the church. The Church needs such forerunners who will announce that the glory of the latter House is greater than the *former house. "The 42nd Generation" is the generation that will "house" the latter glory. May you increase in wisdom and stature, as these important mysteries of Christ are revealed to you.*

Dr. Sagie Y. Govender – ABC Ministries; South Africa
Senior Minister, Antioch Christian Tabernacle
Founder and Presiding Apostle , ABC Ministries.
www.apostolicleader.co.za

The 42nd Generation is a powerful and revolutionary unveiling of the present day body of Christ in the earth. Dr. Kiwi S. Kalloo sounds a clear voice giving us a precise blueprint for this generation. The detailed account of scripture and the effective application makes this writing a catalyst for both transformation and demonstration. The truth contained here is imperative for the overcomer and essential for our victorious journey. You will find woven within the words of this book the spirit of impartation that will establish present truth and quicken the heart.

Cathy Walker
Pastor, Greater Dimensions Church
President and Founder, Revolution Online School
www.cathywalker.org
cathy@cathywalker.org

I am happy to submit the following endorsement: In his book, "The 42nd Generation", Kiwi has gone to great lengths to remind us of an important truth. From God's revelation of the creation of man in Genesis, God illustrated that He is a Generational God. When we renew our relationship with God through salvation, we discover the power of influencing future generations. I recommend this book as it will challenge you to deepen your relationship with God and impact your generations.

Dr. Richared Pinder
Pastor/Sr. Vice President
Bahamas Faith Ministries Fellowship
Bahamas Ministries International

When I first became acquainted with brethren teaching the Feast of Tabernacles, it opened a vast world of new spiritual understanding. It was also very important for the upgrade our Heavenly Father was presenting to us in that season. Most of the esteemed apostles and prophets serving the purpose of God at that time addressed many subjects that the Pentecostal community knew very little about. One of them was the matter of the 42nd generation. Many of us were challenged to count the names in the genealogical listing in Matthew 1. When we did, we discovered there were only forty-one names listed including Jesus Christ. At first, that presented somewhat of a challenge. Where was that stealth 42nd generation? We came to understand that the 42nd generation was a people in Christ - a seed coming forth out of His loins in every generation. To my knowledge, tracts, chapters in books, and small articles were written on this subject but never a full treatment. Kiwi Kalloo has boldly ventured into deep waters to present a treatise on this powerful subject. He has merged together a variety of metaphors describing this people in Christ. I would encourage each of you who read this seminal treatment to meditate carefully on each subject and each chapter. One will find a vast array of seed thoughts, and one will find that there's a general connectedness of many ideas in the New and Old Testaments. It is the honor of every son to search the scriptures to see the concealed things revealed. Hear the heart of Kiwi Kalloo in this writing and may each of you be blessed richly as you encounter the 42nd generation.

Dr. Stephen Everett
Pastor and Author
Ph.D and Th.D

There is a new season coming to the church—the apostolic season—in which the emphasis is the call for the church to return to biblical design. Such design appears in Scripture where God's family, the church, is designed to function as the family of God in the earth: a family of sons portraying the image and likeness of the eternal Godhead. For the church to effectively function as the corporate son, it is imperative that it grows up into the fullness of the image of Christ. The maturation of the church is, in principle, the unveiling of the 42nd generation, "the sons of Jesus." Dr. S. Kiwi Kalloo skillfully expounds upon the mystery of the 42nd generation. He unveils the hidden designs locked up in the biblical *typology and presents an intriguing picture of the emerging end-time church in the earth today.*

Apostle Dr. Yasser Rivas
Senior Pastor,
Congregración Cristiana
Santiago, Dominican Republic

I am so happy to be a part of this project. Dr. S. Kiwi Kalloo has devoted his life and life experiences of study and experience with God. On the topic on fatherhood from the revelation of the 42nd Generation he has truly expressed the heart of God and His love for His sons.

This book is filled with life transforming information for the preservation of the future of mankind. From the perspective of fathers and sons, it is truly expressed that we are the sons of God and that there is an expectation of greatness that is perceived by the world. We strive to understand ourselves. In the midst of our venture through life, we find ourselves when we find God. There is no greater love, no greater power, or no greater purpose than that of coming to the full understanding of who we are in Christ.

Our world is struggling with identity and is slowly becoming fatherless. Our children are becoming more and more anti-God and losing hope. This book expresses the ideologies, concepts, and principles of the Kingdom as no other can identify with. It shows us where we came from, where we are currently, and where we are going. It is important for us to understand fatherhood and sonship because it is the cause of life and the plan of God

This book of the 42nd generation is a must read and I am personally recommending to the world that it is eye opening, life transforming, and informative. I stand behind the contents of this book and the author who is a spiritual son. He is a director under my organization: the ACADEMY OF UNIVERSAL GLOBAL PEACE. I am a proud father who stands by his faithful son.

His Eminence Most Rev. Dr. Madhu Krishan, DD; FICA; SD(USA); Ph.D (USA). Founder & Chairman of A U G P (Academy Of Universal Global Peace (http://www.augp.edu.in/) -A Higher Educational & Spiritual unit of Snahalaya Ashram-www.snahalayaashram.com) (AUGP ia an ISO 9001-2008 Certified & Accredited Organization by the United Kingdom)

UNITED NATIONS Global Compact

WE SUPPORT

WE SUPPORT: UNIVERSALLY ACCEPTED 10 PRINCIPLES OF *UNITED NATIONS Global Compact*,

And UNITED NATIONS HUMAN RIGHTS & ALL CHARTERS OF UNITED NATIONS

We Are Affiliated / Registered With

The UNITED NATIONS Academic Impact;

UNITED NATIONS (DESA); UNITED NATIONS Global Compact & EUROPEAN COMMISSION

[As International / Global Organization; Institution & Academy]

Table of Contents

Chapter One
A Seed for a Generation 20

Chapter Two
The Order of the Generations 26

Chapter Three
Three Stripes 30

Chapter Four
The Missing Generation 37

Chapter Five
The Seed of Jesus 40

Chapter Six
The Seed and the First Born 45

Chapter Seven
A Chosen Generation 48

Chapter Eight
Building Zion 52

Chapter Nine
New Jerusalem 56

Chapter Ten
Many Sons to Glory 59

Chapter Twelve
Rights to the Tree of Life 65

Chapter Thirteen
Christ – The Many-Membered Body 70

Chapter Fourteen
Seed of Abraham... 75

Chapter Fifteen
Kingdom of our Lord and His Christ... 78

Chapter Sixteen
Caught Up to the Throne of God.. 81

Chapter Seventeen
The Right Hand of God... 86

Chapter Eighteen
The Son of Man... 90

Chapter Nineteen
What is Man?... 93

Chapter Twenty
Sons Subject to the Father... 97

Chapter Twenty One
The Mark for the Prize Part One... 102

Chapter Twenty Two
The Mark for the Prize, Part Two... 111

Chapter Twenty Three
The Mark for the Prize, Part Three... 117

Chapter Twenty Four
Healing of the Feet.. 124

Biography Profile... 127

Honors.. 129

PREFACE

By

Dr. David C. Yankana

In the world we live in there is a great struggle when it comes to understanding who we are, where we come from, and where are we going. Humanity is suffering from an identity crisis. As a result of not being able to answer these age old questions, mankind has determined in his quest to answer these questions and bring satisfaction to his longing appetite to know the purpose for his existence. This desire has led him to embark on a treasure hunt to discover his true identity.

During his search to know his true identity, man has been impregnated by ideas that have developed into concepts that determine his perception and interpretation of life and his identity. He is faced with a danger, though: when one is impregnated with wrong concepts, his understanding will be inaccurate and incomplete. You can only understand properly if your concepts are in alignment with your ideas, which must be based upon God's dynamic truth.

In the Bible, Satan approached Jesus and asked a pertaining question after Jesus was in the desert for forty days. Satan asked, "[…] if you be the son of God turn this stone to bread" (Matthew 4:3). This question was asked to see if Jesus, who claims to be the son of God, actually believed that he was the son of God, It did not, however, pertain to his ability to turn the stone into bread.

The strength that Satan possesses comes from the fact that we, who are sons of the kingdom of God, don't understand who he is and his position in Christ.

This book, *The 42 Generation*, has a wealth of revelation, concepts, and principles that are found in the Bible. These great insights and profound truths that helps from the lay person to those in prestigious positions in understanding who they are, why are in this world, and where they are going.

The writer has worked as a master craftsman putting the intrinsic pieces together, fittingly framing block by block of revealed truths to bring a greater awareness of who we are and, most of all, whose we are. When we live knowing these profound truths the enemy of our soul will not have the victory over our lives and our world. When truth prevails, the lies and deception will be dispelled by the light it brings. Therefore, man will now be able to reflect the image of God through their life and the by the way he lives.

The writer also lets us know that Jesus is the example—the prototype of what God desire for all His children. He wants us to be like Jesus, kings and priests having the authority on the earth and to faithfully represent His government on this side of heaven. He desires for us to be sons that represent His love, grace, and mercy to a world of people stumbling in the darkness of not knowing who they are and who He is or even of His Kingdom.

This work of the writer called *The 42 Generation* is a must read. It also affords the readers saved time because of the comprehensive research compiled by Dr. S. Kiwi Kalloo in this book. He presents step-by-step learning of vital truths that bring us into a greater understanding of who were are as sons of the Kingdom of God.

Romans 8 declares that the earth mourns and groans for the manifestation of the sons of God. This is the time that we all come to this place of understanding that we are the corporate son on the earth—called to make a difference.

Dr. David C. Yankana
Sr. Pastor
Kingdom Life Ministries

FOREWORD

By

Dr. R. Pepe Ramnath

I am so happy that you have decided to read this book. Dr. S. Kiwi Kalloo has given the best of his writing with tireless research on this great topic on fatherhood from the revelation of the 42nd Generation.

This book contains information for the preservation of the future of mankind. Everything a man would ever need to become a Father is already inside of him. Man was wired, structured, and engineered by the ultimate Father and designer to be the best Father he could ever possibly be. If we were designed to be Fathers then why are we failing so terribly? This book would reveal this mystery and save our dying generations to come.

It seems like our world is slowly becoming Fatherless and our children are becoming more and more aimless with less possibilities of changing. A child that seems to have his or her life together is forced to become lawless quickly, in order, to be accepted by their peers. The absence of a Father only helps to enhance this pressure that our children feel.

Life is made simple through the instructions of our creator. If we were to carefully study and obey these instructions life would become simple, predictable, and full of joy. *The 42nd Generation* will enlighten you and elevate you to defeat the disease of fatherlessness that has so plagued this present generation. So many have abandoned their call and walked away from God through selfish acts of ignorance. Ignorance has been Satan's greatest weapon for he is the prince of this domain call darkness. In order words, it is more costly and expensive to be ill informed than to be well learned.

Dr. S. Kiwi Kalloo has spent many years learning and working with some of the greatest minds that have graced the earth to compile this book. He has carefully written this literature with beautiful cross references of the original language for your growth and development. I highly recommend this reading to a people who desire to preserve a generation that would carry out the creator's order of Fatherhood. May

God enlighten and increase you as you read this great text straight from the heart of the author and his desire for the preservation of humankind.

Dr. R. Pepe Ramnath, Ph.D
Pastor/Author/Research Scientist
Miramar Kingdom Community Center

INTRODUCTION

The 42nd Generation is based on treasured truths written by the leading of the Holy Spirit and the grace of the pen. God is today revealing Himself to His sons and daughters as never before. As we press on to know Him we are coming to know more about ourselves, who we are, and what we were born to be. As the world today experiences darkness and loss of identity, there is a revelation that is taking place within the body of Christ. God is calling upon His sons to take their rightful place and build His Kingdom.

Throughout this book I have used the original King James Version of the Bible, the Blue Letter Bible Online, and the English Dictionary for major references and research.

Throughout this book I have expressly used the Hebrew Alphabet along with numbers and their meanings pertaining to truth and the revealing of God's Word.

Every letter of the Hebrew Alphabet has a significant meaning and a numerical value that brings out truth that expresses the heart of God and His plan for His sons on the earth and in His Kingdom. Hebrew letters are read from the right to the left and are comprised of 22 letters in its Alphabet.

To fully understand truth we must come to a place where we can lay aside all that we have inherited from our Father's and the past Generations. We must lay aside the arm of the flesh and lean on the arms of the Father and allow him to speak from His heart to our hearts.

Based on *Strong's Exhaustive Concordance of the Bible*, I have used the Hebrew letters, words and their meaning to capture the greater picture of the meaning of a word, along with the numerical value of the letters and the meaning of the numbers; thus, showing their significance and how relevant it is to us today in the Kingdom of God.

I have also placed the actual scripture verses to help the reader to be able to capture the message; and, to not be distracted by researching and flipping pages to see if what is written is scripturally correct.

The 42nd Generation is based on a message that speaks about the identity and glory of the Sons of Jesus who make up the 3rd and final Generation of Priests. The sons of God who become one with Jesus, and, as they come into the light of His Glory they will shine just like the son who is Jesus because they will be the Generation of Jesus Christ.

Chapter One
A Seed for a Generation

Psalms 22:30-31 KJV
[30] A <u>seed</u> shall serve him; <u>it shall be accounted to the Lord for a generation.</u>
[31] They shall come, and shall declare his righteousness unto a people that shall be born, that he hath done this.

Seed: Strong's H2233 - *zera`* זֶרַע zeh'·rah
seed, sowing, offspring, descendants, posterity, children

ZAYIN: the 7th letter of the Hebrew Alphabet that speaks of a weapon that cuts off and is represented by the #7, which speaks of perfection.

RESH: The 20th letter of the Hebrew Alphabet that speaks of the head, the highest person in authority, the leader. The #20 speaks of the blood, even the blood that remits sin, and is represented by the #200 which speaks of the insufficiency of man, showing that he is fallible and needs God.

AYIN: The 16th letter of the Hebrew Alphabet that speaks of an eye, to know, see, look, manifest, make visible. The #16 speaks of love. Represented by the #70 which speaks of perfect spiritual order, and God is bringing his many sons into His perfect divine order.

Seed, as expressed in the Hebrew Alphabet, represents an offspring and an extension of the tree from which it came. Man who is insufficient by himself and unable to redeem himself, is loved by God beyond his faults. He is looked upon through the eyes of grace. Through grace, man has been redeemed and bought with a price, knowing that regeneration must take place. Through this process, there will be a cutting away of the flesh that will bring us unto perfection and the perfect spiritual order of God.

A seed is that which possesses vital force or life-giving power. A seed is the vehicle of regeneration and rebirth.

Galatians 3:29
[29] *And if ye be Christ's, then are ye Abraham's seed, and heirs according to the promise.*

The Word says that if we belong to Christ or Jesus, the anointed one, then we qualify as the seed of Abraham and heirs to the promises of God. The first thing shown here is that Jesus is the seed of Abraham. Through Jesus, we have been grafted into the promise as heirs according to the promise. So that makes us sons of the promise and if we are His sons, then we are the seed of Jesus.

Generation: Strong's H1755 – *dowr* דּוֹר dōre: A life cycle of seeds measured over a period of time.

In terms of years, one generation is roughly 30 among human beings, accepted as the average period between the birth of parents and the birth of their offspring. This is the process of bringing into being; production or reproduction, especially of offspring.

Here is the beauty of God's word. If the term of years for a generation is 30 years then we must understand that the #30 speaks of maturity. According to Jewish customs, when a man child enters manhood his father will take him out before the elders and all the city and throw a great feast to declare to all:

"Today my son has become a man. He is now become of age and is now qualified to do business in my name. Whatever my son declares will be law, because when you see my son you will see me".

On the flipside of that, until a son grows up and becomes a man he would not have been fronted by his father and pronounced to be a full grown son. Until he has grown up, he will not be able to get into covenant with a wife and produce seed that will be counted as a generation.

Mary, who was espoused to Joseph, was found to be with child of the Holy Ghost, not knowing any man. Mary, who is a woman, is typical of the church and the Holy Spirit is that same spirit of the Father who has planted His seed within the earth of her womb. That seed took root out of the earth, or the womb of Mary, and a man child or a seed came forth.

That same seed went through the process of life and was buried at the hands of men. In three days after that same seed died, it brought forth many seeds out of one, by faith. That seed had to stay buried for three days because it takes three days for a seed to die.

In that same three days that Jesus was buried within the earth, it was typical of Him being planted or buried within the hearts of men, so that after the three days that same seed could multiply and regenerate, bringing forth new life by his death.

Genesis 15:18
[18] *In the same day the* LORD *made a covenant with Abram, saying, Unto thy seed have I given this land, from the river of Egypt unto the great river, the river Euphrates:*

Egypt speaks of distress, hard labor, death, darkness, and barrenness. And the Lord promised Abraham that he would give unto his seed the land that borders the river Euphrates which speaks of fruitfulness. Salvation from barrenness to fruitfulness is what the Lord had promised Abraham and to his seed.

Genesis 3:15
[15] *And I will put enmity between thee and the woman, and between thy seed and her seed; it shall bruise thy head, and thou shalt bruise his heel.*

Revelation 12:17
[17] And the dragon was wroth with the woman, and went to make war with the remnant of her seed, which keep the commandments of God, and have the testimony of Jesus Christ.

This enmity has its origins in Genesis 3:12 between the devil and the woman because it takes the man to sow seed and the woman to bear fruit. So if the seed is destroyed there will be no fruit

John 12:24
[24] Verily, verily, I say unto you, except a corn of wheat fall into the ground and die, it abideth alone: but if it die, it bringeth forth much fruit.

Unless a seed falls into the ground and dies, it will not be able to multiply but will remain alone. If it dies, however, it will bring forth much fruit. Since we are the seed, the best thing the enemy can do with us is bury us. The most powerful place for the seed is in the ground. The most dangerous thing to do with a seed to place a seed in the ground, then bury and leave it there to die.

However, it is the design of God that when a seed is placed into the ground and dies, that it births new life. A tree is born with the ability to reproduce new seed in abundance that will come forth through fruitfulness.

Jesus, the seed of Abraham, was beaten, left for dead, put into a tomb of earth. After three days, He rose from the dead and reproduced many seeds, which are called sons, the many members of the body of Christ, the sons of Jesus, the seed of Jesus, and the seed that will be counted for a generation.

The Romans thought that the best place to keep the body of Jesus was in the tomb—and they were right. See, when a seed dies and rises in newness of life, it protrudes out of the earth where it was buried and is made evident to all by the testimony or the living proof of life that it has risen from death.

Hebrews 2:16-17
¹⁶ For verily he took not on him the nature of angels; but he took on him the seed of Abraham.
¹⁷ Wherefore in all things it behoved him to be made like unto his brethren, that he might be a merciful and faithful high priest in things pertaining to God, to make reconciliation for the sins of the people.

Jesus took on him the seed of Abraham, he was made like unto his brethren that he might be merciful and faithful as the high priest of God, pertaining to his brethren and to make reconciliation for the sins of his people.

Romans 4:13-16
¹³ For the promise, that he should be the heir of the world, was not to Abraham, or to his seed, through the law, but through the <u>righteousness of faith.</u>
¹⁴ For if they which are of the law be heirs, faith is made void, and the promise made of none effect:
¹⁵ Because the law worketh wrath: for where no law is, there is no transgression.
¹⁶ Therefore it is of faith, that it might be by grace; <u>to the end the promise might be sure to all the seed;</u> not to that only which is of the law, but to that also which is of the faith of Abraham; who is the father of us all,

It was indeed because of the righteousness of faith and not the promise; it is of faith by grace that the promise will be made sure to all the seed. For if it was by the law then we would all be judged and without hope, but by faith we are saved through grace and not of ourselves.

Romans 9:8
⁸ That is, they which are the children of the flesh, these are not the children of God: <u>but the children of the promise are counted for the seed.</u>

Galatians 3:14-16
[14] *That the blessing of Abraham might come on the Gentiles through Jesus Christ; that we might receive the promise of the Spirit through faith.*
[15] *Brethren, I speak after the manner of men; Though it be but a man's covenant, yet if it be confirmed, no man disannulleth, or addeth thereto.*
[16] *Now to Abraham and his seed were the promises made. He saith not, And to seeds, as of many; but as of one, And to thy seed, which is Christ.*

The promise was through faith and of one seed which is Christ, the many sons of Jesus.

Galatians 3:26-29
[26] *For ye are all the children of God by faith in Christ Jesus.*
[27] *For as many of you as have been baptized into Christ have put on Christ.*
[28] *There is neither Jew nor Greek, there is neither bond nor free, there is neither male nor female: for ye are all one in Christ Jesus.*
[29] *And if ye be Christ's, then are ye Abraham's seed, and heirs according to the promise.*

We who are Christ's; who belong to Christ are the seed of Abraham, according to the promise. Because Jesus died, he had many sons through seed, time, and harvest that brought forth fruits.

Chapter Two
The Order of the Generations

1ˢᵗ 14 Generations
Matthew 1:1-16
¹*The book of the generation of Jesus Christ, the son of David, the son of Abraham.*
²*Abraham begat Isaac; and Isaac begat Jacob; and Jacob begat Judas and his brethren;*
³*And Judas begat Phares and Zara of Thamar; and Phares begat Esrom; and Esrom begat Aram;*
⁴*And Aram begat Aminadab; and Aminadab begat Naasson; and Naasson begat Salmon;* ⁵*And Salmon begat Booz of Rachab; and Booz begat Obed of Ruth; and Obed begat Jesse;*
⁶*And Jesse begat David the king; and David the king begat Solomon of her that had been the wife of Urias;*

2ⁿᵈ 14 Generations
Matthew 1:7-11
⁷*And Solomon begat Roboam; and Roboam begat Abia; and Abia begat Asa;*
⁸*And Asa begat Josaphat; and Josaphat begat Joram; and Joram begat Ozias;*
⁹*And Ozias begat Joatham; and Joatham begat Achaz; and Achaz begat Ezekias;*
¹⁰*And Ezekias begat Manasses; and Manasses begat Amon; and Amon begat Josias;*
¹¹*And Josias begat Jechonias and his brethren, about the time they were carried away to Babylon:*

3ʳᵈ 13 Generations
Matthew 1:12-16
¹²*And after they were brought to Babylon, Jechonias begat Salathiel; and Salathiel begat Zorobabel;*
¹³*And Zorobabel begat Abiud; and Abiud begat Eliakim; and Eliakim begat Azor;*
¹⁴*And Azor begat Sadoc; and Sadoc begat Achim; and Achim begat Eliud;*

¹⁵And Eliud begat Eleazar; and Eleazar begat Matthan; and Matthan begat Jacob;
¹⁶And Jacob begat Joseph the husband of Mary, of whom was born Jesus, who is called Christ.

1ST Order   2nd Order   3rd Order

ABRAHAM	SOLOMON	SALATHIEL
ISAAC	ROBOAM	ZOROBABEL
JACOB	ABIA	ABIUD
JUDAS	ASA	ELIAKIM
PHARES	JOSAPHAT	AZOR
ESROM	JORAM	SADOC
ARAM	OZIAS	ACHIM
AMINADAB	JOATHAM	ELIUD
NAASSON	ACHAZ	ELEAZAR
SALMON	EZEKIAS	MATTHAN
BOOZ	MANASSES	JACOB
OBED	AMON	JOSEPH
JESSE	JOSIAS	JESUS
DAVID	JECHONIAS	**CHRIST-MANY MEMBERED BODY**

Melchizedek = "my king is Sedek" (King of Righteousness)
Salem means "Righteousness & Priest of Jehovah"
Melchizedek is none other than God himself.

Genesis 14:18-20
¹⁸And Melchizedek king of Salem brought forth bread and wine: and he was the priest of the most high God.
¹⁹And he blessed him, and said, Blessed be Abram of the most high God, possessor of heaven and earth:
²⁰And blessed be the most high God, which hath delivered thine enemies into thy hand. And he gave him tithes of all.

Psalms 110:4
⁴The LORD hath sworn, and will not repent; Thou art a priest for ever after the order of Melchizedek.

The Bible was uniquely written with a numerical value to every word. The number fourteen speaks of Melchizedek priesthood.
The number 14 is = 7 x 2
7 speaks of perfection.
7 = 6 + 1

6 is the number of man, the flesh.
1 is the number of God for he is one God.
1 + 6 = a God man, becoming one with him just as he and the Father are one.
Man coming to perfection.

2 speaks of a testimony.
Every 14 Generation God did something significant that changed the world.
14 x 3 = 42
14+14+14 = 42

3 speaks of completion because God is a triune being, Father, Son and Holy Spirit.

 The lineage of Abraham to Jesus added up to 41 Generations. A generation can only be carried on through a particular bloodline. The physical bloodline stopped at Jesus and the only way for this Melchizedek priesthood to come forth is through the firstborn son of Jesus who will make up the last and final generation.

 So we have been called to be Kings and Priests unto God. If the number 14 speaks of a Melchizedek, and the number 3 speaks of completion, and the number 2 speaks of a testimony and the number 7 speaks of perfection and the number 6 speaks of man.

 It all points to one thing: the number 42 or the 42nd Generation speaks of and represents one new man (6) who had been through an experience with God (1) and has overcome and been perfected (7) with the testimony of Jesus Christ (2) after the order of the priesthood (14) and will make up the one new man in Christ who has been made complete after the image of the heavenly (42).

He is the One who is the King of righteousness without beginning or end of days.

I know that it sounds confusing but it not a matter of figuring out anything, it is a matter of hearing what the Spirit is speaking. Through this type of revelation the Holy Spirit is showing us the path that we should walk to get to him.

Jesus did not just have one son but he had many firstborn sons, a body with many members who are overcoming and on their way to perfection, to take their rightful place as Kings and Priests before God and all nations of the world. We are that 42nd Generation of God, or what some refer to as the missing Generation. We are known as the firstborn among many brethren, the man-child, the overcomer, the Joshua Generation, a Generation of the sons of God.

Jesus begot many sons through the woman, who is the church, and they are coming forth in Revelation 12 as the overcomers.

Chapter Three
Three Stripes

According to Old Testament law, 13 lashes is the maximum punishment that is allowed.

The **#13** speaks of the limit of the law and Jesus met that requirement. In so doing so, He fulfilled the law.

WHIP
The whip that was used to beat Jesus was made of two pieces of ox skin and one piece of the skin of an ass.

OX
1st Piece of OX skin **(Servanthood)**
2nd Piece of OX skin **(A Testimony)**
1 Piece of Ass skin **(The Adamic Nature)**

The one piece of ox skin represents the servant-hood of man. The second piece represents confirmation of his testimony and ability to become a Cherub through service to the Master. (A Cherub is one who carries the Glory)

ASS
The one piece of ass skin represents the old Adamic carnal nature in us that needs to be broken and brought under the subjection of the spirit through ripping, tearing and suffering.

3 RIPPING HOOKS (One Whip)
The #3 speaks of completion (Father, Son & Holy Spirit)
The #13 speaks of the limit of the law (Jesus was the 13th son of his generation)

The #39 speaks of disease in the feet (the last part of the body that comes out when one is born). The feet are now being restored with strength by the Word and lifted up by the Hand Ministry which is the Five-Fold Ministry.

WOMAN
Speaks of the church

FEET
Speaks of the last part of the body that is born out of the woman at child birth

MANCHILD
Speaks of the overcomers, the sons of Jesus, the brethren of Jesus, the first born sons of God, the 42nd Generation

Jesus took upon his back 13 lashes that made 39 stripes upon his body. As the sons of Jesus, we are required to bear that one last lash that will create three stripes upon our humanity. Each stripe serves a purpose: one for the Spirit; one for the soul; and and one for the body, giving the triune man complete healing.

$13+1 = 14$
The #14 speaks of Melchizedek priesthood, a generation of priests and Kings unto God.

To fully consummate this covenant someone will have to bear three stripes.

$39+3 = 42$
The #42 speaks of the 42nd generation, the generation of Jesus Christ, the many sons of Jesus.

3 STRIPES
Father, Son and Holy Ghost

1 LASH
The mark for the prize of the high calling that is in Christ Jesus

Philippians 3:10
¹⁰ That I may know him, and the power of his resurrection, and the fellowship of his sufferings, being made conformable unto his death;

Romans 12:2²
And be not conformed to this world: but be ye transformed by the renewing of your mind, that ye may prove what is that good, and acceptable, and perfect, will of God.

When Jesus was pierced on his side, blood and water flowed out.

BLOOD
The life of Christ in us

Poured out upon the earth (flesh, man) his life is being poured out upon man.

WATER
The Word which is spirit and life

In the beginning was the Word and the Word was with God and the word was God (John 1:1). His word is being written upon the fleshly tablets of our hearts.

3 BECOMING ONE
One lash, 3 stripes
One God, 3 offices

John 17:21-22
²¹ That they all may be one; as thou, Father, art in me, and I in thee, that they also may be one in us: that the world may believe that thou hast sent me.
²² And the glory which thou gavest me I have given them; that they may be one, even as we are one:

The #1 speaks of God

א Alef: The first letter in the Hebrew alphabet; Speaks of an ox or bull = strength, primacy, leader. Represented by the #1 which speaks of God

Genesis 1:1
¹ In the beginning God created the heaven and the earth.

John 1:1
¹ In the beginning was the Word, and the Word was with God, and the Word was God.

This foot company is being birthed and is coming forth without disease, strength is being poured in so that we could stand against the wiles of the devil and do exploits for our God.

Acts 3:1-8
¹ Now Peter and John went up together into the temple at the hour of prayer, being the ninth hour.
² And a certain man lame from his mother's womb was carried, whom t hey laid daily at the gate of the temple which is called Beautiful, to ask alms of them that entered into the temple;
³ Who seeing Peter and John about to go into the temple asked an alms.
⁴ And Peter, fastening his eyes upon him with John, said, Look on us.
⁵ And he gave heed unto them, expecting to receive something of them.
⁶ Then Peter said, Silver and gold have I none; but such as I have give I thee: In the name of Jesus Christ of Nazareth rise up and walk.
⁷ And he took him by the right hand, and lifted him up: and immediately his feet and ankle bones received strength.
⁸ And he leaping up stood, and walked, and entered with them into the temple, walking, and leaping, and praising God.

PETER & JOHN
2 witnesses—speaks of a testimony.

This means that he who was diseased in his feet from birth is being looked upon and he is being raised up from his infirmity; disease and weakness on the ninth hour, 3:00 o' clock.

3:00 PM is the 9th hour of the day.

This man with the diseased feet speaks of all humanity that was born in sin and shaped in iniquity.

The **#9** speaks of fruitfulness

So this man who is being raised up will bear fruit so that the husbandman can come into his garden, the church, and eat of this fruit and find pleasure in his harvest.

At the scourging of Jesus, when he was beaten for all humanity, allowing the blood to flow unto the earth, with his flesh being ripped apart into bits and pieces as he endured the agony and pain of the flogging, becoming the perfect sacrifice for our redemption. His blood flowing and falling on the earth was symbolic of His blood through faith falling upon our fleshly hearts and minds being earthly.

In the Old Testament, the maximum lash according to the law that any human being could receive for a crime that was worthy of condemnation was thirteen—thirteen agonizing lashes. The number thirteen, therefore, speaks of the limit of the law. Jesus is the 13th generation from the carrying away into Babylon.

The whip consisted of three sprang of animal skin and three very small hooks made up of a very sharp object. The animal skin used was one piece of ass skin and two pieces of ox skin. The ass skin speaks of the old Adamic carnal nature of man, the rebelliousness and disobedience of man. The one piece of ox skin speaks of servant-hood, while the other piece of ox skin speaks of a confirmation, testimony, and the ability to become a Cherub through service.

The small hooks placed on each end of the animal skin were strategically incorporated for the purpose of ripping and cutting the flesh. Every time Jesus received one stroke of the whip, it amounted to three stripes and the total amount of strokes that Jesus received was thirteen. 13X3=39.

The number 39 speaks of disease in the feet and Jesus took the maximum beating that was permitted by law.

We are the last church age, the last part of the body that is being born out of the woman. The woman represents the church. In childbearing, the last part of the body that comes out of the woman is the feet.

So there is a foot company that is being born out of the church (woman). This foot company is also called the overcomer, the man-child, the one new man in Christ, the brethren of Jesus, the 42nd generation, the remnant, and the elect of God. This foot company is a company of sons who will not bow to the image of Baal.

Jesus is a direct descendant of Abraham, being the 41st generation from Abraham. Thus, we are the sons of Jesus which make up the 42nd generation.

The 42nd generation is a King Priest generation of sons who have overcome and have become perfect and one with God. Jesus went to the limit of the law which is 39, leaving one lash of the whip—equal to three stripes—yet to be received. 39+3=42. The whip that we must endure is an experience with God and the testimony of His son.

The limit of the law was 13 because 14 would equal death. Jesus the head received 13 and we, the body, are taking on one which is 13+1=14. The number 14 speaks of a Melchizedek priesthood and a King Priest generation. Jesus said that we must die to live. In other words, we must suffer to reign. The number 3 speaks of completion and the one stroke of the three stripes will perfect us in God. To fully consummate this new covenant, we must bear the final three stripes in the spirit. Our triune man must experience God in fullness.

Philippians 1:21
[21] *For to me to live is Christ, and to die is gain.*

The number 3 speaks of fullness, completion, and perfection. The stripes were necessary to allow the blood and water to flow out of the body of Jesus and fall to the earth (man). The one stroke that we must bear is the working of the Holy Spirit. The number 1 speaks of God and the 3 stripes which we will receive on account of the 1 strike is that of the working of a triune God, Father, Son and Holy Spirit which speaks of the fullness of God. This will ultimately represent the manifestation of the fullness of Christ forever.

Throughout the past generations, the sons of men were born with disease in their feet because the sons were not born of the will of God, but of the will of the flesh. There is a birthing taking place today and God is bringing forth a company of sons, who are born out without disease and their hands are loose and not withered.

We are being ripped apart and God is dividing the light from the darkness; the spirit from the flesh. God is setting a standard of true holiness and godliness. His many sons are coming to glory and perfection by enduring the cross just as Jesus did. The man-child is coming to glory. We are that man-child, the sons of God.

Chapter Four
The Missing Generation

Continuing to speak about the 42nd Generation, we have come to an understanding that David was number 14. Jechonias was also number 14. Joseph, the husband of Mary, was number 40, making Jesus number 41 which is the 13th one on the 3rd list (13 generations from the Babylonian captivity).

As we have seen and read and come to know that the King Priest Generation is number 14, we see that Jesus was the 13th who had no son to carry on the genealogy and bloodline. Well, let's pay special attention to what the Bible says about this. He was Jesus the Christ. Christ, as we know, is the many-membered body which is spoken of in Corinthians. This 42nd Generation is the many-membered body of Christ, not Jesus alone but His sons also.

Matthew 1:17
17 So all the generations from Abraham to David are fourteen generations; and from David until the carrying away into Babylon are fourteen generations; and from the carrying away into Babylon <u>unto Christ</u> are fourteen generations.

Verse seventeen says that from Abraham to Christ is forty-two generations. Christ makes up the company of the Sons of God who have been born again and washed in the blood of the Lamb and have put on the Lord Jesus Christ and now bear the mind of Christ. Jesus was the 13th and we are the 14th Generation. We are the Generation who has been chosen and called to become Kings and Priest unto God after the order of Melchizedek.

God is bringing forth a company of sons from the nations of the world, a glorious company of sons after the image of his Son Jesus. This is the Generation of Jesus Christ, the elect company, called out of all ages and all generations, those who are the true seed of Abraham. Who are now heirs and joint heirs with Christ, who will rule and reign with him on His throne with our Father David.

1 Corinthians 12:12
¹² For as the body is one, and hath many members, and all the members of that one body, being many, are one body: so also is Christ.

1 Corinthians 12:27
²⁷ Now ye are the body of Christ, and members in particular.

    The book of I Corinthians tells us that we are the body of Christ. Though we are many, we are all one with Christ in God. The truth is we are not missing, but we are in the making. God is making a man in the express image of his son, Jesus. That man is the man-child who will rule the nations with a rod of iron: the overcomer, the sons of God.

Revelation 21:7
⁷ He that overcometh shall inherit all things; and I will be his God, and he shall be my son.

    Revelation says that we, who press toward the mark for the prize and overcome, will inherit all things. The word "all" means with the exception of none. We read in John 1 that all things were made by Him. We also read in the Gospels that the meek shall inherit the earth. We know that all things come from God and we also know that God is above all, through all, and in all.

Hebrews 2:13
¹³ How shall we escape, if we neglect so great salvation; which at the first began to be spoken by the Lord, and was confirmed unto us by them that heard him;

Romans 8:29
²⁹ For whom he did foreknow, he also did predestinate to be conformed to the image of his Son, that he might be the firstborn among many brethren.

What a glorious truth: before the beginning of the world, we were thought of by God to be the firstborn among many who would be directly in line to receive a double portion blessing.

As we are conformed to the image of His Son we are becoming one with Him, just as He and the Father are one. We have been grafted into the natural olive branch and now we have royal blood running through our veins. We are heirs and joint heirs with Christ, we are the sons of God, the 42nd Generation, the King Priest Generation, the body of Christ.

Chapter Five
The Seed of Jesus

Isaiah 53:8-10
⁸ *He was taken from prison and from judgment: and who shall declare his generation? for he was cut off out of the land of the living: for the transgression of my people was he stricken.*
⁹ *And he made his grave with the wicked, and with the rich in his death; because he had done no violence, neither was any deceit in his mouth.*
¹⁰ *Yet it pleased the LORD to bruise him; he hath put him to grief: when thou shalt make his soul an offering for sin, he shall see his seed, he shall prolong his days, and the pleasure of the LORD shall prosper in his hand.*

In the Old Testament, when a man had a son, they celebrated the birth of an heir, a seed, someone to carry on his genealogy and legacy. It was devastating to any man who could not bring forth seed. Jesus did not marry nor did he have any physical children, yet Isaiah said "he shall see his seed, and shall prolong his days." This points to Jesus as having a son, one who will be able to carry on the legacy of his Father.

Some have read this scripture and interpret this as though Jesus was married to Mary Magdalene and had a son. Well, let us get enlighten on the heart of the Father. Jesus came in the flesh and did not get married in the flesh (that's all hog wash). He has been espoused to one wife who has been found with child of the Holy Ghost, and that holy thing which shall be born of her shall be called the Son of God. The woman, the church, has been pregnant with the son of God for many months now and she is travailing to give birth to this man-child.

She is approaching her ninth month to give birth and the Joseph ministry has been protecting and accommodating her. There is no room in the inn of the hearts of the organizations and the programs and the systems of this world. Strangely enough, she is finding refuge in the house of the servants - the manger where the serving animals are kept.

We have learned how to plan so well that not even God could become a member of our well organized system. The entire creation groans and waits for the manifestation of the sons of God. While the woman has found safety in the house of the servant, Herod seeks to kill the child before he is born. There is a spirit of Herod that has come into the church and seeks to kill the man-child or anything that looks or sounds like it.

This spirit has entered into the hearts of pastors and ministers. They have been blinded by the veil that has covered their eyes. Tradition and religion have taken over and the harlot system and the carnal mind have taken over. We have a form of godliness, but we deny the power of God (II Timothy 3:5). We have become so full of ourselves that when the Lord comes to us and our place of worship, we lock him out and call Him false because the things that He is speaking does not sound like what we are teaching. The way He dresses and walks is different from us so that makes him false.

We have hewn out for ourselves cisterns to produce water but that water does not proceed out of the belly of God. The strange thing about a living spring is that it comes out of the source and flows wherever it will. It does not flow uphill, but downhill. Wherever the earth chooses to accommodate ponding, the running water would use the opportunity to fill that pond and continue to pass through it and to overflow into other ponds and valleys.

This spirit of Herod crept in unawares and has put a blindfold over the eyes of our leader. This spirit likes to be in control; does not know how to delegate; and overpowers its coworkers. It likes to micromanage and when things go bad, quickly points fingers to blame others, never admitting to faults or mistakes. This spirit does not have a reputation for raising leaders.

It feels threatened of losing control and power. True leaders are not given a chance to grow around this type of spirit.

This Herod spirit is a ministry killer, no real true ministry stands a chance under such a spirit. In the midst of the dictatorship and suppression, there is a ministry of wise men who will support and build with the sons. The wise men ministry sees the star and follows after it in support of the light of it. The star speaks of ministry and new life.

Herod also sees the star and defies the purpose of the star because Herod wants to be the star. Herod does not want this star to shine because the star will take all the attention from him. We are the seed of Christ and the very thing that He had to go through is what we will also find ourselves going through. We are special to God, but also a threat to Herod.

Jesus sees His seed and will prolong his days but someone besides God is also watching. That someone is the spirit of anti-anointing, the spirit of anti-Christ, the spirit of Herod. The firstborn son is the only one who could ascend the throne by inheritance; the firstborn is a threat to the throne of Herod. When a star (ministry) is born, it is seen by both the wise men and Herod. The wise men will make their way to the star to support and honor the King, but Herod will also send spies who will disguise themselves as wise men pretending to support and honor the star.

We must be able to hear what the angel is speaking, as the angel is the messenger from the heart of God. The Bible says that when the Comforter is come, He will lead us into all truths, we can only be able to distinguish between the two by the Holy Spirit. Only the Spirit of Truth can lead us into truth.

John 16:7,13
7Nevertheless I tell you the truth; It is expedient for you that I go away: for if I go not away, the Comforter will not come unto you; but if I depart, I will send him unto you.

13 Howbeit when he, the Spirit of truth, is come, he will guide you into all truth: for he shall not speak of himself; but whatsoever he shall hear, that shall he speak: and he will shew you things to come.

Something like the truth is not truth. Truth is such a thing that when you see it, you will know it; when you hear it, you will know it; when you have come in contact with it, you will know that it is different from the rest. When Jesus met the woman at the well, she ran around town declaring to all, "come, see a man". She had an encounter with truth, for God is truth.

The woman with the issue of blood heard about this Jesus so she pressed until she touched the hem of His garment. She also had an encounter with the King of all the earth. Truth is contagious. It is inspiring and breathes hope. It speaks life and brings an end to tradition. Truth brings change wherever it goes.

Truth is never threatened, because truth cannot change. We change and will continue to change and be transformed, as we conform to the revelation of truth. Every seed will produce after its own kind. He shall see his seed, and his seed will spring up into a new life and bear fruit after its own kind. Jesus was born after a full term of nine month; nine, being the number of fruitfulness. When the man-child is fully matured, he will bear the nature of his father.

He will carry his father's name. His name speaks of his nature and character. We are the 42nd Generation and we are not missing, as rumored, but are in the making. Mary, the mother of Jesus, riding upon an ass brings forth a tremendous truth. The woman speaks of the church, while ass speaks of the carnal mind or the flesh.

All over the world in the local church, the body of Christ, there is a body of people who are hearing from God and have taken the journey of the ass nature, or the flesh. They are making their way to the manger to give birth to this man-child. This is the true message of the Kingdom. It comes in righteousness, peace, and joy in the Holy Ghost.

Romans 14:17
17 For the kingdom of God is not meat and drink; but righteousness, and peace, and joy in the Holy Ghost.

The 42nd Generation is the Kingdom Generation, the Generation of Jesus Christ.

Chapter Six
The Seed and the First Born

Psalms 22:30-31 KJV
³⁰ A seed shall serve him; it shall be accounted to the Lord for a generation.
³¹ They shall come, and shall declare his righteousness unto a people that shall be born, that he hath done this.

Psalms 22:30-31 AMP
³⁰ Posterity shall serve Him; they shall tell of the Lord to the next generation.
³¹ They shall come and shall declare His righteousness to a people yet to be born--that He has done it, that it is finished

There is a Generation that will come forth and walk in His righteousness upon the earth, showing a people that shall be born, what the Lord can do. This ministry is a ministry of reconciliation that will follow the Master across the Jordan, lay their lives down, and get rid of the old man at the Jordan. This ministry, or son-ship company, will lay their lives down so that they may take it back up.

This seed company, as described in verse 30, will follow the Lord across the Jordan, which speaks of death to the carnal man. The seed company will put on the mind of Christ, taking up the mantle or the robe of the master, receiving a double portion of His spirit. This signifies that He has received the blessing and inheritance of a firstborn son. The seed company will journey back across the Jordan looking like the Master and walking in the authority of the Master. He will make his way back to the place where he left his brethren, the sons of the Prophets who were viewing from afar off.

The book of Psalms says that a seed shall serve Him. Which seed? It is the seed which He himself had planted in the earth and in the hearts of a company of sons shall serve Him. This seed shall be accounted for as a Generation unto the Lord, the Generation of Jesus Christ—the 42nd Generation.

The sons of the prophets served and believed in the same God, but did not journey over the Jordan. All they saw, or were able to see, was the Master being taken away.

They did not see an inheritance. They did not see the blessing of the firstborn. They did not witness the final work of the Master, and that the work was finished. The seed, the Elisha Company, had to come back and declare the finished work: to a people that were yet to be born; a people whose mind was not transformed; a people who did not work out their salvation with fear and trembling.

This seed was planted deep down so that it was able to shoot upward. Jesus said, "he that exalts himself shall be abased, but he that humbles himself shall be exalted" (Matthew 23:12). This seed, or Generation of sons, will bear fruit that is identical to the Master and the fruit will be that of the fruit of the Spirit.

Isaiah 61:9-11
⁹And their seed shall be known among the Gentiles, and their offspring among the people: all that see them shall acknowledge them, that they are the seed which the LORD hath blessed.
¹⁰ I will greatly rejoice in the LORD, my soul shall be joyful in my God; for he hath clothed me with the garments of salvation, he hath covered me with the robe of righteousness, as a bridegroom decketh himself with ornaments, and as a bride adorneth herself with her jewels.
¹¹ For as the earth bringeth forth her bud, and as the garden causeth the things that are sown in it to spring forth; so the Lord GOD will cause righteousness and praise to spring forth before all the nations.

This seed shall be known among the gentiles and be blessed of the Lord. Out of the gentile nations of the world, God is calling forth a company of sons who will make His name known and be blessed of the Lord. God is forming a new generation of son—the

Generation of Jesus Christ, the righteous seed. Even the offspring of this seed shall be known and blessed of God.

This company of sons will be clothed with the robe of righteousness and the garment of praise, causing the garden to spring forth and bud even like Aaron's rod that budded. It's the King Priest Generation, the 42nd Generation, coming forth in the glory of the Father. Jesus went down to the river Jordan to be baptized of John. When He came up out of the water, a voice spoke from heaven saying, "this is my beloved son in whom I am well pleased" (Matthew 3:17).

There is a calling to the sons of God to lay down the flesh and the carnal mind. The sons of God are called to be clothed with Christ, rising up into a new creation for old things are passed away and behold all things have become new. That new man is the one new man in Christ who will be conformed to the image of his son, bearing the new name and nature of Jesus Christ. Putting off the old, which is corruptible and putting on the new which is incorruptible.

Chapter Seven
A Chosen Generation

1 Peter 2:9
⁹ But ye are a chosen generation, a royal priesthood, an holy nation, a peculiar people; that ye should shew forth the praises of him who hath called you out of darkness into his marvelous light:

Here is the highlight of the promises of God. He said that we are exceptionally blessed as:

1. A chosen Generation
2. A royal priesthood
3. A holy nation
4. A peculiar people

We are a chosen generation, the Generation of Jesus Christ, the 42nd Generation, a King Priest Generation, a Generation of sons, called out from every nation of the world. We are a royal priesthood because we have been called to offer our sacrifices continually before Him. Through grace we now have the blood of Jesus, the King, flowing in our veins. We are a holy nation, because we are called to be holy and blameless before God in all things. We are called to be a peculiar people, because peculiar means to be distinctive in nature and character from others.

God has called forth a people to be different in nature and character from the status quo to which we are accustomed by putting on the nature and character of Jesus Christ. We are called forth with a purpose to show His praises.

Praises flows continuously from man. We were designed as an instrument of praise. Our praises were intended to go up unto God and no one else. We have strayed from our original intent and our praises have been diverted to another. God through Jesus Christ is reconciling the world back unto himself and when we arrive and fully get to God, our praises will be fully focused on Him alone.

His Work of Grace

1. Called out of darkness
2. Called into his marvelous light.

The light, which is Jesus, did shine and still shines like the son into our hearts. When God created the heavens and the earth, darkness was upon the face of the deep. That deep referred to was the heart of man that was void and without form. So God is speaking to our hearts today and it is taking on the form of Jesus Christ and we are being transformed into the image of the heavenly. According to Genesis 1:2, "the earth was void and without form and darkness was upon the face of the deep."

The heavens were not void and without form, but the earth "man." We have been called into His marvelous light for He is light.

Romans 8:29
[29] *For whom he did foreknow, he also did predestinate to be conformed to the image of his Son, that he might be the firstborn among many brethren.*

1. Foreknown by God
2. Predestinated to be
3. Conformed to the image of his son
4. Firstborn among many brethren

Before the foundation of the world began, we were known by God and predetermined to take on the image of His son to become the firstborn among many brethren, a body with many members.

Ephesians 1:4
⁴According as he hath chosen us in him before the foundation of the world, that we should be holy and without blame before him in love:

    1. Chosen us in him
    2. Before the foundation of the world
    3. To be holy
    4. To be without blame
    5. To be before him in love

Ephesians 1:5
⁵ Having predestinated us unto the adoption of children by Jesus Christ to himself, according to the good pleasure of his will,

    1. Predestinated us
    2. The adoption of children by Jesus Christ to Himself
    3. The good pleasure of His will

It is the will of the Father that we become His own. The Father takes pleasure in calling us His own, so He adopted us who were afar of. We were castaways and strangers, but He adopted us to become His own sons and daughters, giving us the right to inherit His throne as His firstborn.

Ephesians 4:13
¹³ Till we all come in the unity of the faith, and of the knowledge of the Son of God, unto a perfect man, unto the measure of the stature of the fullness of Christ:

    1. Till we all come
    2. In the unity of the faith
    3. The knowledge of the son of God
    4. Unto a perfect man
    5. Unto the measure
    6. Of the stature
    7. Of the fullness of Christ

We are called with a purpose: to become one with the Father. There is, however, a process to perfection; process takes time. "Til" is a time word, telling us that our natural abilities cannot complete this process. We will need to come to the unity of the faith, the knowledge of the son of God, and perfection.

We are all given a measure which will bring us to stature that takes us to fullness. Yesterday, today and forever, good, acceptable and perfect will of God. The components of the Tabernacle—the Outer Court, Holy Place, and Holy of Holies—are analogous to our whole person (spirit, soul, and body) and the Holy Trinity (Father, Son, and Holy Spirit).

Isaiah 43:5-7
5 Fear not: for I am with thee: I will bring thy seed from the east, and gather thee from the west;
6 I will say to the north, Give up; and to the south, Keep not back: bring my sons from far, and my daughters from the ends of the earth;
7 Even every one that is called by my name: for I have created him for my glory, I have formed him; yea, I have made him.

1. Bringing the seeds from the east, west, north and south.
2. Sons from afar and daughters from the ends of the earth
3. Called, created, formed and made for His glory

God is gathering His seed from around the world, from the nations of the world and every tribe and every tongue. He is gathering the 42nd Generation who will rule the nations with a rod of iron. We are called for fullness, ultimately to inherit God.

Chapter Eight
Building Zion

God has commissioned me to write and speak this word, this message of the Kingdom, not as a proof text to truth or to try to convince the unbeliever or the cold-hearted Christian who is satisfied with the measure and status-quo. This message of the Kingdom is intended for those of us who are hungry to become matured in God, to get to the higher realms of the Spirit and, ultimately get to the heart of the Father, to become one with Him and to be filled with all of Him.

Many generations have come and gone throughout the history of man, but God has a special interest in one generation: the one that He has written about from Genesis to Revelation; the one that He is perfecting into the image of His son. The ZION of God.

There is a day when the Lord is about to return in His Glory. He is coming in clouds that are full of water which will pour themselves out on the earth. Clouds in the Bible speak of ministry; water speaks of the Word; and the earth speaks of man. Jesus is coming in a ministry, in a people that are full of the Word of life who will speak this Word to the nations.

We need to answers to the following questions: Who are we? Why are we here? How did we get here? Where we are going?

Psalms 102:12-16
[12] *But thou, O LORD, shalt endure for ever; and thy remembrance unto all generations.*
[13] *Thou shalt arise, and have mercy upon Zion: for the time to favor her, yea, the set time, is come.*
[14] *For thy servants take pleasure in her stones, and favor the dust thereof.*
[15] *So the heathen shall fear the name of the LORD, and all the kings of the earth thy glory.*

[16] *When the LORD shall build up Zion, he shall appear in his glory.*

God is building His house not out of wood and stones, but out of flesh. The scriptures declare that the tabernacle of God is within men. We are the temples of the most high God. The Bible says that unless the Lord builds the house, they that labor, labor in vain. This house, like the Ark and like the Tabernacle, is being built upon the foundation of the Apostles and Prophets. The dimension of this house has been set by numbers and limitation. God is building this house. His plan is very specific and He is the sole occupant. This house will be a holy city, the new Jerusalem, which is coming down from God, mansions and holy vessels. The chief cornerstone of this house is none other than Jesus. The foundations of this house are built upon truth, righteousness, peace, and joy in the Holy Ghost.

Before the Lord comes, He will first build up Zion and then his glory will be expressed through Zion. This Zion spoken of here is the overcomer: the one new man in Christ, the 42nd generation, the man-child, the foot company, the Elisha generation, the company of firstborn sons.

God is getting us ready to express His glory, nature, and character. He is making known unto us His ways, just like He did with Moses. The greater work that Jesus spoke of will be manifested in us and through us.

When Jesus raised Lazarus from the dead, he eventually died. There is coming a day when the dead in Christ shall rise and will die no more, for death and hell have been conquered and Jesus holds the keys in his hands. The sting of death, which is sin, has been cut off. Jesus has injected into our veins His blood, which is the antidote for the poison of sin.

Psalms 102:17-21
[17] *He will regard the prayer of the destitute, and not despise their prayer.*
[18] *This shall be written for the generation to come: and the people which shall be created shall praise the LORD.*

19 For he hath looked down from the height of his sanctuary; from heaven did the LORD behold the earth;
20 To hear the groaning of the prisoner; to loose those that are appointed to death;
21 To declare the name of the LORD in Zion, and his praise in Jerusalem;

Verse 18 spoke about us, the generation to come, a people which shall be created to declare his praises in Jerusalem.

Hebrews 2:14-18
14 Forasmuch then as the children are partakers of flesh and blood, he also himself likewise took part of the same; that through death he might destroy him that had the power of death, that is, the devil;
15 And deliver them who through fear of death were all their lifetime subject to bondage.
16 For verily he took not on him the nature of angels; but he took on him the seed of Abraham.
17 Wherefore in all things it behoved him to be made like unto his brethren, that he might be a merciful and faithful high priest in things pertaining to God, to make reconciliation for the sins of the people.
18 For in that he himself hath suffered being tempted, he is able to succour them that are tempted.

Jesus did not take on the form of angels, but that of the seed of Abraham. He is a kinsman redeemer, the root of Jesse, the Lion of Judah, the Judge of Israel, Messiah of Israel, the hope of David, the true olive branch. He is the faithful high priest who offered up a worthy sacrifice to redeem man and to see His seed and to prolong His days. This Jesus of Nazareth did not have one son, but many. These many sons make up the many-membered body of Christ, the generation of Jesus Christ.

The Lord is coming back, not to be spit upon, beaten or crucified but to appear in His glory.

Zion is that special place called the Holy of Holies, the third heaven, behind the veil, a place of fullness and unlimited glory of God. We are that place which God has designated for His habitation. He is now in the process of building and furnishing this house. We are to take His abode forever and ever.

Chapter Nine
New Jerusalem

Revelation 21:2
² *And I John saw the holy city, new Jerusalem, coming down from God out of heaven, prepared as a bride adorned for her husband.*

Jerusalem was built as a city, the City of God. It is built on seven hills, but the highest of these hills is where David's throne rested. This was known as Zion. The voice of the King was heard from this place and the law went forth out of Zion.

It appears that God has been working in the same fashion throughout time from generation to generation. Moses went up to the mountain, a very high place, where he heard the voice of the King. There is a high place in the spirit where God speaks and we are able to hear His voice. The Psalmist David said, "he that dwelleth in the secret place of the most high shall abide under the shadow of the Almighty" (Psalm 91:1). The Most High can only dwell on high.

God cannot lower His standards. Though He came low down to man on earth in the form of flesh, just like man, even then He said "my will is to do the will of him that sent me" (John 6:38). **Jesus said, "I am not my own, but I belong to my Father which is on high."** Paul said, "no man ought to think more highly of himself than he is" (Romans 12:3).

It is not a matter of thinking high, but coming to a place where we can look and see through the Spirit, Jesus on high. See Him not as our standard of earthly, fleshly, and carnal understanding and behavior, but see Him as the King who is dwelling upon the highest mountain of Jerusalem, the City of God. See Him as He speaks to the nations establishing His Kingdom on the earth and in the heart of man, who is being changed into the image of the heavenly.

Revelation 2:9-10
⁹ And there came unto me one of the seven angels which had the seven vials full of the seven last plagues, and talked with me, saying, Come hither, I will shew thee the bride, the Lamb's wife.
¹⁰And he carried me away in the spirit to a great and high mountain, and shewed me that great city, the holy Jerusalem, descending out of heaven from God,

This new Jerusalem, this holy City, the Lamb's wife, the overcomer, the bride of Christ is found in the Zion of God. It is the highest realm of the Spirit. Those who sit on the throne to rule and reign with Him, not everyone in the church has this place, it is for HIM that overcomes. They are known as His brethren, conformed to His image, to which He will declare His Father's name.

Psalms 22:22
²² I will declare thy name unto my brethren: in the midst of the congregation will I praise thee.

God is declaring His name which speaks of His nature unto His brethren, the overcomers. God will glorify them and show His praises in the midst of this gathering or congregation as we know it.

Hebrews 2:12
¹² Saying, I will declare thy name unto my brethren, in the midst of the church will I sing praise unto thee.

God is singing a song over the chosen, it is called prophetic, which means "from God." This praise of God is a declaration of son-ship. When Jesus came up out of the water at the Jordan, the Father spoke in declaration "this is my beloved son in whom I am well pleased" (Matthew 3:17). One who has received power and authority from the Father to do business in His name (nature) with a ring on his finger and a robe upon his back was given to him by the Father.

Romans 8:29
²⁹ For whom he did foreknow, he also did predestinate to be conformed to the image of his Son, that he might be the firstborn among many brethren.

We are called to be sons through blood transfusion. We were accepted in the beloved and have been called to be a part of this firstborn of the brethren, one who will journey to the Jordan and back to minister to his brethren. We are a Kingdom Priest Generation, the 42nd generation, the brethren of Jesus Christ.

God is forming man, the brethren of the Lord and body of Christ, after the nature and character of our Lord Jesus Christ. We are that firstborn son who will receive a double portion of His spirit and inheritance. We are the ones who will live on and carry on the name of our Father. We will inherit the throne and reign as Kings and Priests declaring His praises among the nations of the world. We are yet servants because the scripture says that a son is not any different from a servant as long as he remains a child (Galatians 4:1). So he is placed under teachers and parental authority and given guidance until he becomes a man, fully matured and grown up. Only then he will be able to take his place on the heavenly throne as heir. My people will be his people and he will rule the nations with a rod of iron. He is the brethren of the Lord.

Chapter Ten
Many Sons to Glory

Hebrews 2:9-11
⁹ But we see Jesus, who was made a little lower than the angels for the suffering of death, crowned with glory and honour; that he by the grace of God should taste death for every man.
¹⁰ For it became him, for whom are all things, and by whom are all things, in bringing many sons unto glory, to make the captain of their salvation perfect through sufferings.
¹¹ For both he that sanctifieth and they who are sanctified are all of one: for which cause he is not ashamed to call them brethren,

The one that sanctifies is Jesus and the ones who are sanctified are the first fruits, the overcomers, the man-child company, the many sons that is coming to glory. He is not ashamed to call them brethren. This company of brethren is the 42nd generation, the seed of Jesus Christ. He is declaring these brethren to be His own before the nations of the world.

Hebrews 2:12-13
¹² Saying, I will declare thy name unto my brethren, in the midst of the church will I sing praise unto thee.
¹³ And again, I will put my trust in him. And again, Behold I and the children which God hath given me.

The children and the brethren are one and the same. They are the seed given for signs and wonders. The sign will tell the world that it is a God thing and the wonders will confirm His presence.

Isaiah 8:18
¹⁸ Behold, I and the children whom the LORD hath given me are for signs and for wonders in Israel from the LORD of hosts, which dwelleth in mount Zion.

Jesus was a sign and a wonder in Israel, but He was not alone. God has given him some children, a seed, accounted to the

Lord for a generation, the "sons of God." This includes His brethren of His early walk on earth as a perfect man who are also His "seed" or offspring or children.

When Jesus poured his precious life out at Calvary, He had an offspring: a seed, children who carried on His name and manifested His life and nature. They were also signs and wonders, the Zion of God, the bride, the Lamb's wife.

John 1:12
¹²But as many as received him, to them gave he power to become the sons of God, even to them that believe on his name:

God is gathering His seed and brethren from the many nations of the world from every tongue and tribe. He is gathering all in one unto himself. To all those He gathers, He is revealing His heart and mind and the manifested glory.

Romans 8:19
¹⁹ For the earnest expectation of the creature waiteth for the manifestation of the sons of God.

There is an expectation and groaning that is taking place in the Spirit and all of creation. This groaning and waiting is for the manifestation of the sons of God which can only take place through the manifestation of the Spirit of God. There is an uncelebrated and hidden expectation within the heart of every man, a longing, even a hope of His appearing.

Romans 8:29
²⁹ For whom he did foreknow, he also did predestinate to be conformed to the image of his Son, that he might be the firstborn among many brethren.

This firstborn and the brethren are also one and the same. He is calling forth a people from a people, a nation from every nation, a company of overcomers, and a people whose destiny is set and has been predetermined by God before the foundation of the world.

It is the Father's good pleasure to see the son come to maturity, when He declares His son to be a man before the nations; it is a sign of seed. When His son acts on His Father's behalf and does business in His name it is counted as a wonder that glorify the Father through the Son.

Having a son means that a seed was born. Through that seed the bloodline will continue and another generation will continue on the name of the Father.

Looking at the way God works, it is the Father, who is God, and then the Son, who is Jesus, and the sons of the Son, who are the many-membered body of Christ. The many-membered body of Christ is coming unto perfection and will carry on His name and nature through the blood of Jesus that is now flowing within the veins of the body of Christ.

Every Father desires his son to follow in his footsteps, through bloodline, through his name, character, personality, and even trade. The fulfillment of this is what makes the Father proud. The son himself is a sign and his stature and workings of society is a wonder as it expresses the nature and characteristics of the Father.

Chapter Eleven
Becoming One with God

II Pet. 1:20
[20] *Knowing this first, that no prophecy of the scripture is of any private interpretation.*

No prophecy is given with a private interpretation that is contradictory to the will of God and His written Word. The scripture says, by "the mouth of two or three witnesses let every word be established" (II Corinthians 13:1). The word established meaning to become of a permanent nature.

God is making a man after His express image and He is bringing this man-child to a place where the nature of God will become permanent in him. God is not working on a temporary fix but a permanent and long lasting fix for man. This fix is for eternity, it is final.

God has set principles when it comes to understanding His Word. Throughout eternity, He cannot change His principles, because His principles are infallible. There is no imperfection in His Word. It does not need to be rewritten; in fact, it was written in parables, types, shadows, and parallels for our maturity and perfection. The scripture says that it is the glory of God to conceal a matter but it is the honor of Kings to seek it out (Proverbs 25:2).

The Word of God has an enormous wealth of treasures that have been hidden from the swine. To conceal means to hide, cover, or disguise. The treasures are the pearls and the swine are the unclean hearts and minds that have not been circumcised and regenerated by the Holy Spirit. These treasures can only be found by following the map of the Word, which God has provided for us to follow.

The map or the Word is very specific in its meaning and purpose and cannot be altered. There is only one route to get to the heart of the Father and that route has a gate and that gate is named Jesus.

If Jesus has brethren, then He is an elder brother. If He has children, a seed to declare His generation, then He must be a father.

I Cor. 2:12-13
[12] Now we have received, not the spirit of the world, but the spirit which is of God, that we might know the things that are freely given to us of God.
[13] Which things also we speak, not in the words which man's wisdom teacheth, but which the Holy Ghost teacheth; COMPARING SPIRITUAL THINGS WITH SPIRITUAL."

This map, although very specific in guiding us to the Father, is also very unique in means and methods. Think of a safari and leading a team of people on an expedition. The very first thing that we will need to acquire is a guide. Basically it is someone who knows the way, someone with experience, who has been there before or knows how to venture into the unknown. This guide is one and the same: the Holy Spirit, of the gospel of John, who will guide us into all truths.

This guide, or Holy Spirit, knows how to read the map or the Word of God. He has been to the place of fullness. He came from the bosom of the Father. In fact, He and the Father are one. His credibility is second to none. Nobody knows the Father better than Him. If our plan is to get to the heart of God, we must first get this guide to guide us. He knows the way. He knows every turn that we must take with the first turn being the turn from sin. He knows every path that we must stay on, and one of those paths is the path of righteousness.

He knows exactly when and where we should rest. That rest is in God. Jesus said, "come unto me all you who are weary and heavy laden, take my yoke upon you and learn of me, for my yoke is easy and my burden is light" (Matt 11:28-29). The yoke is easy because He took it upon himself and the burden is upon Him. So if we come to Him and accept Him into our hearts, there is no more price to be paid because He paid it all.

Isaiah 9:6
⁶ *For unto us a child is born, unto us a son is given, and the government shall be upon his shoulder: and his name shall be called Wonderful, Counselor, the mighty God, THE EVERLASTING FATHER, the Prince of Peace.*

Isaiah declared to all that the child was also a son, and the government shall be upon His shoulders. Shoulders representing authority, thus God's divine government being upon Him. His name or nature is Wonderful, Counselor, The mighty God, everlasting Father, Prince of Peace. They all are one and the same. Jesus is the everlasting Father and we are His sons.

He is the 41st generation. From Abraham and His sons will make up the 42nd generation. God will not stop at 41 because it just does not make a perfect man.

6 is the number of man and 6x7 is 42, six is the number of man and 7 is the number of perfection. So Jesus was one generation short of God making a perfect man in Christ.

Jesus is the Son of the God of heaven and if we accept Him and become His sons, then He will make us perfect, just as He is perfect as the everlasting Father who is in heaven.

Chapter Twelve
Rights to the Tree of Life

Every father longs for his son to grow up and become a man, knowing that he came from the loins of his father. The father knows that his son will carry on his name and represent him wherever he goes.

My physical Father was a very well known man in Trinidad. People everywhere knew that he had a good heart. He would take in homeless and unfortunate people and bring them into our home and make them part of our family. He stood up for what was right in the community, even though he was a very rough man. Wherever I would go throughout Trinidad and people heard my name I would immediately be recognized as the son of Benji or Kalloo.

We are branded and recognized by association, which could be good or bad, but ultimately we want to be identified with Jesus. We live in a society today where people crave positions and titles, but even amid all these positions and titles if we do not have Christ, we have nothing. Our society today suffers from an identity crisis: many people do not know who they are and are trying to be like someone else.

Well, let me declare to you that God made each and every one of us unique; it does matter if our gifts and talents are similar to others. There is only one you. Before the foundations of the world began, God knew you. God knows the number of hairs that are on our head. He knows us by name, even if we are known to the world by the same name.

To God we are known on an individual basis. There is only one you and there will never be another you. When we come to God and find Him, it does not make us dumb or clueless. In fact, only then can we fully come to the realization of who we are.

The purpose of a thing is determined by its maker. We were designed for greatness with the ability to become like God.

God made man in His image and likeness. Adam was sinless and a son of God—an heir of God. But he believed in a lie, the lie that the devil told Eve to tell him. The devil told Eve that in the day that she opened her mind up to the knowledge that was fruitful on the tree of the knowledge of good and evil, that her eyes would be opened.

Here is the thing: her physical eyes were already opened and her perception of God was all light. Though she was already made in the image and likeness of God, the devil corrupted her mind by telling her that she was not like God; though she was an heir of God. For the first time she conceived the sin of doubt and believed in a lie and spoke the same to her husband, Adam, who also believed it. Judicially, through the process of being born again, we are one with Him, bear His glory, and declare His nature and character.

In our experience, we have not yet attained the prize. We are yet to overcome and receive the prize. God has always intended for man to be like Him and to share in His glory. Hebrews 11:6 says, "[…] without faith, it is impossible to please God." Adam and Eve lost faith and believed in another, who gave to them a corrupted word which corrupted their minds, making their minds became carnal. They chose to believe the lie of not being like God instead of believing the truth that they were made in the image and likeness of God.

Revelation 1:7-8
⁷ Behold, he cometh with clouds; and every eye shall see him, and they also which pierced him: and all kindreds of the earth shall wail because of him. Even so, Amen.
⁸ I am Alpha and Omega, the beginning and the ending, saith the Lord, which is, and which was, and which is to come, the Almighty

He is coming with clouds, a great cloud of witnesses: Moses and Elijah. Every eye shall see him—both the believer and unbeliever. They that rejected him shall mourn and lament very bitterly because of their ignorance. Jesus declared that He was the Alpha and Omega, the first and last, and which is to come, the Almighty. He was declaring that He and the Father are one.

Revelation 22:12-14
¹² And, behold, I come quickly; and my reward is with me, to give every man according as his work shall be.
¹³ I am Alpha and Omega, the beginning and the end, the first and the last.
¹⁴ Blessed are they that do his commandments, that they may have right to the tree of life, and may enter in through the gates into the city.

The gates into the city are the same as the door to heaven, or the ladder that Jacob saw. These gates represent the order of God that bring people to a place of perfection, who, through partaking of the tree of life, will live and reign with Him forever.

Revelation 21:6-7
⁶ And he said unto me, It is done. I am Alpha and Omega, the beginning and the end. I will give unto him that is athirst of the fountain of the water of life freely.
⁷ He that overcometh shall inherit all things; and I will be his God, and he shall be my son.

He that is thirsty will drink freely and the overcomer shall inherit all things as Jesus will be his God and he will be the son of God.

Ephesians 4:11-13
¹¹ And he gave some, apostles; and some, prophets; and some, evangelists; and some, pastors and teachers;
¹² For the perfecting of the saints, for the work of the ministry, for the edifying of the body of Christ:
¹³ Till we all come in the unity of the faith, and of the knowledge of the Son of God, unto a perfect man, unto the measure of the stature of the fulness of Christ:

Revelation 3:21
[21] To him that overcometh will I grant to sit with me in my throne, even as I also overcame, and am set down with my Father in his throne.

Jesus and the Father are one and the same and cannot be separated.

Luke 17:8-10
[8] For I have given unto them the words which thou gavest me; and they have received them, and have known surely that I came out from thee, and they have believed that thou didst send me.
[9] I pray for them: I pray not for the world, but for them which thou hast given me; for they are thine.
[10] And all mine are thine, and thine are mine; and I am glorified in them.

John 17: 21-23
[21] That they all may be one; as thou, Father, art in me, and I in thee, that they also may be one in us: that the world may believe that thou hast sent me.
[22] And the glory which thou gavest me I have given them; that they may be one, even as we are one:
[23] I in them, and thou in me, that they may be made perfect in one; and that the world may know that thou hast sent me, and hast loved them, as thou hast loved me.

Our main purpose is to get to the Father through transformation; to become one with him.

Isaiah 8:18
[18] Behold, I and the children whom the LORD hath given me are for signs and for wonders in Israel from the LORD of hosts, which dwelleth in mount Zion.

Ephesians 1:9-10
[9] Having made known unto us the mystery of his will, according to his good pleasure which he hath purposed in himself:
[10] That in the dispensation of the fullness of times he might gather together in one all things in Christ, both which are in heaven, and which are on earth; even in him:

Colossians 1:27

²⁷ *To whom God would make known what is the riches of the glory of this mystery among the Gentiles; which is Christ in you, the hope of glory:*

Colossians 2:9-10
⁹ *For in him dwelleth all the fullness of the Godhead bodily.*
¹⁰ *And ye are complete in him, which is the head of all principality and power:*

Psalms 22:22
²² *I will declare thy name unto my brethren: in the midst of the congregation will I praise thee.*

Psalms 102:21
²¹ *To declare the name of the LORD in Zion, and his praise in Jerusalem;*

Hebrews 11:39-40
³⁹ *And these all, having obtained a good report through faith, received not the promise:*
⁴⁰ *God having provided some better thing for us, that they without us should not be made perfect.*

The better things to come for the body of Christ is coming to perfection and becoming one with Him.

Chapter Thirteen
Christ – The Many-Membered Body

Colossians 1:26-28
²⁶ Even the mystery which hath been hid from ages and from generations, but now is mafe manifest to his saints:
²⁷ To whom God would make known what is the riches of the glory of this mysery among the Gentiles: which is Christ in you, the hope of glory:
²⁸ Whom we preach, warning every man, and teaching every man in all wisdom; that we may present every man perfect in Christ Jesus:

The hidden truths or mysteries which were hidden from the previous generations and ages are now being revealed and are becoming a reality to the body of Christ today. The same body of Christ or the sons of God is coming into the reality of the riches of His glory among the gentiles. Christ in you, not in heaven, is the hope of glory. The hope of this glory is to present every man perfect in Christ Jesus.

I Corinthians 12:12-22
¹² For as the body is one, and hath many members, and all the members of that one body, being many, are one body: so also is Christ.
¹³ For by one Spirit are we all baptized into one body, whether we be Jews or Gentiles, whether we be bond or free; and have been all made to drink into one Spirit.
¹⁴ For the body is not one member, but many.
¹⁵ If the foot shall say, Because I am not the hand, I am not of the body; is it therefore not of the body?
¹⁶ And if the ear shall say, Because I am not the eye, I am not of the body; is it therefore not of the body?
¹⁷ If the whole body were an eye, where were the hearing? If the whole were hearing, where were the smelling?
¹⁸ But now hath God set the members every one of them in the body, as it hath pleased him.
¹⁹ And if they were all one member, where were the body?
²⁰ But now are they many members, yet but one body.

²¹ And the eye cannot say unto the hand, I have no need of thee: nor again the head to the feet, I have no need of you.
²² Nay, much more those members of the body, which seem to be more feeble are necessary.

The body consists of many parts, which make the body unique. Psalm 119:14 says that the body is "fearfully and wonderfully made" after the image and likeness of God. There are many members within this one unit: Jesus, the head and we, the body.

1 Corinthians 12:27
²⁷ Now ye are the body of Christ, and members in particular.

The natural body is one with many members, so also is Christ. There are many members, but one spiritual body. When each member finds its rightful place and begins to function in accordance with its intent of design, the entire body will have become perfect.

Colossians 1:18-22
¹⁸ And he is the head of the body, the church: who is the beginning, the firstborn from the dead; that in all things he might have the preeminence.
¹⁹ For it pleased the Father that in him should all fulness dwell;
²⁰ And, having made peace through the blood of his cross, by him to reconcile all things unto himself; by him, I say, whether they be things in earth, or things in heaven.
²¹ And you, that were sometime alienated and enemies in your mind by wicked works, yet now hath he reconciled
²² In the body of his flesh through death, to present you holy and unblameable and unreproveable in his sight:

Jesus, who is the head of the body and the church, is also the firstborn from the dead. All things are now accountable to Him who conquered death and the grave, proving that the antidote for the sting of sin and a permanent vaccination from the effects of sin when Christ is fully formed in us.

Colossians 1:18-22 (Amplified Bible)
[18] *He also is the Head of [His] body, the church; seeing He is the Beginning, the Firstborn from among the dead, so that He alone in everything and in every respect might occupy the chief place [stand first and be preeminent].*
[19] *For it has pleased [the Father] that all the divine fullness (the sum total of the divine perfection, powers, and attributes) should dwell in Him permanently.*
[20] *And God purposed that through (by the service, the intervention of)Him [the Son] all things should be completely reconciled back to Himself, whether on earth or in heaven, as through Him, [the Father] made peace by means of the blood of His corss.*
[21] *And although you at one time were estranged and alienated from Him and were f hostile attitude of mind in your wicked activities,*
[22] *Yet now has [Christ, the Messiah] reconciled [you to God] in the body of His flesh though death, in order to present toy holy and faultless and irreproachable in His [the Father's] presence.*

The Amplified Bible explains, in a very unique way, that we are reconciled to be presented faultless and irreproachable in the presence of the Father.

Ephesians 1:22-23
[22] *And hath put all things under his feet, and gave him to be the head over all things to the church,*
[23] *Which is his body, the fulness of him that filleth all in all.*

Jesus is the head of the body, which is the church. He is bringing His body to the reality of the state of the head and the body is yet to experience the fullness which the head has already experienced. Jesus by Himself is not the whole body. Without us, He is only the head. He traded his physical body on the tree of the cross for a many- membered body, which could only be formed by the faith of the son of God.

John 12:24
[24] *Verily, verily, I say unto you, Except a corn of wheat fall into the ground and die, it abideth alone: but if it die, it bringeth forth much fruit.*

John 12:24 (Amplified)
²⁴ *I assure you, most solemnly I tell you, Unless a grain of wheat falls into the earth and dies, it remains [just one grain; it never becomes more but lives] by itself alone. But if it dies, it produces many others and yields a rich harvest.*

    The Amplified Bible really expresses the mind of God about the grain of wheat. By itself it remains alive and alone but, if it buries itself in the earth and dies, it yields a great harvest. From One, many are born. The many brethren; saints of God; the Bride of Christ; the overcomers; the man-child; many sons of glory; and the firstborn of many brethren have the hope of His glory being revealed in them by expressing the nature and character of the Father.

Ephesians 4:15-16
¹⁵ *But speaking the truth in love, may grow up into him in all things,which is the head, even Christ:*
¹⁶ *From whom the whole body fitly joined together and compacted by that which every joint supplieth, according to the effectual working in the measure of every part, maketh increase of the body unto the edifying of itself in love.*

    Every part of the body is fitly joined together and makes increase and edifies itself, with the hope of growing up into Him in all things, even Christ.

Ephesians 4:15-16 (Amplified)
¹⁵ *Rather, let our lives lovingly express truth [in all things, speaking truly, dealing truly, living truly]. Enfolded in love, let us grow up in every way and in all things into Him Who is the Head, [even] Christ (the Messiah, the Anointed One).*
¹⁶ *For because of Him the whole body (the church, in all its various parts), closely joined and firmly knit together by the joints and ligaments with which it is supplied, when each part [with power adapted to its need] is working properly [in all its functions], grows to full maturity, building itself up in love.*

    This body of many members is the brethren of Jesus—the saints and overcomers—who are pressing toward the mark for the prize of the high calling that is in Christ Jesus. When the body has come to perfection, just as the head that has already been perfected, this will be the final finished work of the Lord in reconciling man back unto himself.

Chapter Fourteen
Seed of Abraham

Galatians 3:16
16 Now to Abraham and his seed were the promises made. He saith not, And to seeds, as of many; but as of one, And to thy seed, which is Christ.

Abraham was righteous before the face of the Lord and God blessed him and his seed forever. This seed was not necessitated by the law, but of the faith of the son of God that came through the generation of Abraham. In John 8:58, Jesus said "Before Abraham was, I Am"; the God who made the heavens and the earth. Abraham came through Him.

John 8:58
58 Jesus said unto them, Verily, verily, I say unto you, Before Abraham was, I am.

Galatians 3:26-29
26 For ye are all the children of God by faith in Christ Jesus.
27 For as many of you as have been baptized into Christ have put on Christ.
28 There is neither Jew nor Greek, there is neither bond nor free, there is neither male nor female: for ye are all one in Christ Jesus.
29 And if ye be Christ's, then are ye Abraham's seed, and heirs according to the promise.

Acts 2:38
38 And Peter answered them, Repent (change your views and purpose to accept the will of God in your inner selves instead of rejecting it) and be baptized, every one of you, in the name of Jesus Christ for the forgiveness of and release from your sins; and you shall receive the gift of the Holy Spirit.

We have come to God through faith in the son of God, believing in Jesus the Christ, the Messiah, the King of the earth, the Almighty, Creator of all, and the Head. Galatians 3:27 established that "For as many of you have been baptized into Christ have put on Christ." This baptism is not a water baptism but a baptism of blood, for it is only the blood of Jesus that is capable of washing sins away and redeeming man.

Galatians 3:27
27 *For as many of you as have been baptized into Christ have put on Christ.*

Water baptism is a sign of repentance unto the Lord, but the baptism of blood takes place when we acknowledge Jesus as the Lord and Savior of the world and our lives. If we confess Him as Lord and Savior then, through faith, we belong to the body of Christ and are heirs to His throne. And if we belong to Christ, then we are Abraham's seed through faith.

Galatians 3:26-29 (Amplified Bible)
26 *For in Christ Jesus you are all sons of God through faith.*
27 *For as many [of you] as were baptized into Christ [into a spiritual union and communion with Christ, the Anointed One, the Messiah] have put on (clothed yourselves with) Christ.*
28 *There is [now no distinction] neither Jew nor Greek, there is neither slave nor free, there is not male and female; for you are all one in Christ Jesus.*
29 *And if you belong to Christ [are in Him Who is Abraham's Seed], then you are Abraham's offspring and [spiritual] heirs according to promise.*

We are being clothed with the Son of God, with the mind of Christ, and His righteousness. We are the offspring of Abraham through the righteousness of Jesus Christ—spiritual heirs according to the promise that God made to Abraham.

Romans 4:16
16 *Therefore it is of faith, that it might be by grace; to the end the promise might be sure to all the seed; not to that only which is of the law, but to that also which is of the faith of Abraham; who is the father of us all,*

We are not justified by the law, but through faith—faith in Jesus Christ who gave Himself for us on the tree of the cross. It is not because of what we have done, but what He has done; not because of our righteousness, because our righteousness is become as filthy rags, according to Isaiah 64:4. "We have all sinned and come short of the glory of God," declares Romans 3:23. The good news is that Jesus endured the cross and gave Himself as a ransom for us to redeem our souls and bring us unto Himself.

Acts 20:32
³² And now, brethren, I commend you to God, and to the word of his grace, which is able to build you up, and to give you an inheritance among all them which are sanctified.

God is building us as vessels of honor. We are being prepared to receive an inheritance and that inheritance is God. So many of us are longing to walk on streets of gold and wear a golden crown; but, I want to provoke you, my brethren, that you should look up and see that God is making us into streets of gold for all of humanity to see His glory in us and to glorify Him.

The crown made of gold is the glory upon our heads and our minds becoming the minds of Christ. The mind of God is the glory of God resting upon us in fullness without measure. We are being made into one, one piece of gold beaten into a usable shape, an instrument of praise by Him, through Him and for Him.

The body of Christ, of which He is the head, is one and Jesus is part of that body. Jesus Christ makes up the one new man in Him: the man-child, the overcomer, the firstborn, the God-man. This all comes through Abraham's seed. We are directly in line to receive an inheritance of becoming one with Him because of the promise that he made to Abraham. We are Abraham's seed.

Chapter Fifteen
Kingdom of our Lord and His Christ

Revelation 11:15
15 And the seventh angel sounded; and there were great voices in heaven, saying, The kingdoms of this world are become the kingdoms of our Lord, and of his Christ; and he shall reign forever and ever.

Our Lord is the Lord of the universe and His Christ. The many-membered body is coming unto perfection and shall reign forever and ever and we shall reign with him.

Revelation 11:15 (Amplified Bible)
15 The seventh angel then blew [his] trumpet, and there were mighty voices in heaven, shouting, The dominion (kingdom, sovereignty, rule) of the world has now come into the possession and become the kingdom of our Lord and of His Christ (the Messiah), and He shall reign forever and ever (for the eternities of the eternities)!

Psalms 2:2-8
2 The kings of the earth take their places; the rulers take counsel together against the Lord and His Anointed One (the Messiah, the Christ). They say,
3 Let us break Their bands [of restraint] asunder and cast Their cords [of control] from us.
4 He Who sits in the heavens laughs; the Lord has them in derision [and in supreme contempt He mocks them].
5 He speaks to them in His deep anger and troubles (terrifies and confounds) them in His displeasure and fury, saying,
6 Yet have I anointed (installed and placed) My King [firmly] on My holy hill of Zion.
7 I will declare the decree of the Lord: He said to Me, You are My Son; this day [I declare] I have begotten You.
8 Ask of Me, and I will give You the nations as Your inheritance, and the uttermost parts of the earth as Your possession

The Amplified declares that the anointed of God was installed and placed as King on the holy hill of Mount Zion. Mount Zion being the over-comers, the 42nd generation of Kings and Priests, who has come unto perfection.

Revelation 2:26-27
^{26} And he that overcometh, and keepeth my works unto the end, to him will I give power over the nations:
^{27} And he shall rule them with a rod of iron; as the vessels of a potter shall they be broken to shivers: even as I received of my Father.

He shall rule the nations with a rod of iron and Christ, the many-membered, body shall also rule and reign with Him in His triumph.

Revelation 2:26-27 (Amplified Bible)
^{26} And he who overcomes (is victorious) and who obeys My commands to the [very] end [doing the works that please Me], I will give him authority and power over the nations;
^{27} And he shall rule them with a sceptre (rod) of iron, as when earthen pots are broken in pieces, and [his power over them shall be] like that which I Myself have received from My Father;

Jesus is doing for the overcomer what the Father did for Him and we are to Jesus what He was to the Father. John 20:21 says, "[…] even as my Father hath sent me, even so send I you."

John 20:21
^{21}Then said Jesus to them again, Peace be unto you: as my Father hath sent me, even so send I you.

Revelation 12:5
^{5}And she brought forth a man child, who was to rule all nations with a rod of iron: and her child was caught up unto God, and to his throne.

Revelation 12:5 (Amplified Bible)
^{5}And she brought forth a male Child, One Who is destined to shepherd (rule) all the nations with an iron staff (scepter), and her Child was caught up to God and to His throne.

Jesus has overcome and we are overcoming. Jesus is ruling and we will rule when we have attained our rightful place in the Kingdom of God.

God is bringing us to a place of perfection as the body of Christ with Him, being Lord, and us, being his body, that is becoming one with Him.

Chapter Sixteen
Caught Up to the Throne of God

The Sons of God will rule the nations with a rod of iron, so they are being "caught up" to the throne of God.

This word "throne" is mentioned 40 times in the book of Revelation, and only15 times in the rest of the New Testament. The word "Throne" means established authority or seat of authority.

Let's take a look at what and where the Throne of God is:

Isaiah 66:1
¹ Thus saith the LORD, The heaven is my throne, and the earth is my footstool: where is the house that ye build unto me? and where is the place of my rest?

Heaven is the Throne of God and earth is His footstool. What house could we possibly build for God? Psalm 27:1 says, "Except the Lord build the house, they that labor, labor in vain that build it […]" It is not about our fancy buildings, as those buildings are for us and not for God, but it is about the house that God is building.

Psalm 127:1
127 Except the LORD build the house, they labour in vain that build it: except the LORD keep the city, the watchman waketh but in vain.

Acts 7:49
⁴⁹ Heaven is my throne, and earth is my footstool: what house will ye build me? saith the Lord: or what is the place of my rest?

Matthew 5:34
³⁴ But I say unto you, Swear not at all; neither by heaven; for it is God's throne:

Psalms 11:4
⁴ The LORD is in his holy temple, the LORD's throne is in heaven: his eyes behold, his eyelids try, the children of men.

If I am reading this correctly, the Word says that God is in His holy temple and His throne is in heaven. We are told by Paul that our bodies are the temples of the living God, and He is now living within us because we are His temples. The same scripture says that He is in His holy temple and we are that temple. We are the tabernacle of God (I Corinthians 3:16).

1 Corinthians 3:16
¹⁶ Know ye not that ye are the temple of God, and that the Spirit of God dwelleth in you?

If God is in heaven and also in His temple at the same time, it means that this tabernacle is the heaven of God. He said that we ought to mind those things that are heavenly. Philippians 2:5 instructs us, "Let this mind be in you, which was also in Christ Jesus." We are seated together with Christ in heavenly places (Ephesians 2:6).

Philippians 2:5
⁵ Let this mind be in you, which was also in Christ Jesus:

There is a progression of the manifestation of God in His temple. The manifestation of God is dependent upon our maturity and ability to accommodate His presence. If our measure is 30 fold, He will only be able to manifest Himself in a 30 fold way. If our stature is 60 fold, He will only be able to manifest Himself in a 60 fold way and if we continue to press beyond the 60 fold with the hope of getting to 100 fold, then He would manifest Himself in a hundred fold way.

30 fold = 1st Heaven, Baptism of Blood.
60 fold = 2nd Heaven, Baptism of the Holy Spirit.
100 fold = 3rd Heaven, Baptism of Fire.

The mystery remains the same and does not need us to justify or to defend it. God came in the flesh of Jesus and He is coming in our flesh in the same manner being overshadowed by the Holy Spirit.

Psalms 103:19
[19] The LORD hath prepared his throne in the heavens; and his kingdom ruleth over all.

What is your level of Kingdom authority? Is it 30 fold? 60 fold? Or 100 fold? Are we ruling the flesh or are we being ruled by the flesh?

Revelation 4:2
[2] And immediately I was in the spirit: and, behold, a throne was set in heaven, and one sat on the throne.

John was in the spirit. And an authority was established in the spirit realm, or the realm of the Father and "One" meaning God was that established authority.

We can imagine a literal chair in the spirit realm and God who is a Spirit sitting on it. But here is the thing, all of this happened in the spirit and God is a Spirit. This means that John could not see a spirit, because a spirit does not have flesh and bones, so a physical chair could not exist in the spirit realm.

But in the spirit realm, there was an established authority of the Father and He sat in that authority and declared to John, the things that were to come and the final triumph of the Son of God.

JEREMIAH 3:17
[17] At that time they shall call Jerusalem the throne of the LORD; and all the nations shall be gathered unto it, to the name of the LORD, to Jerusalem: neither shall they walk any more after the imagination of their evil heart.

Jerusalem, as we know it in the physical, is a place in Israel. Can you imagine that small city holding about three billion people?

At that time, the city of God—the spiritual Jerusalem—shall be called the authority of God, for they shall be filled with the glory of God. All the nations of the world shall gather themselves unto this holy City of God and call upon the name of the Lord. They shall change their ways and turn from the wicked imagination of their hearts and shall not walk in that way anymore.

There is coming a day, when the Church of Jesus Christ will be the seat of authority, the throne of God, and will manifest His power and His authority in His people. Then all the nations of the world will come to the church, to walk in the light of the glory of God.

Jeremiah 49:38
[38] *And I will set my throne in Elam, and will destroy from thence the king and the princes, saith the LORD.*

ELAM means "high" or the place of the highlands.

Acts 2:9
[9] *Parthians, and Medes, and Elamites, and the dwellers in Mesopotamia, and in Judaea, and Cappadocia, in Pontus, and Asia,.*

On the day of Pentecost, there were many other tongues present, but God chose to refer to Elam because Elam represents a high place in God—the hundred fold, the Jerusalem of God.

The Throne of God is not a literal chair for someone to sit in, but it is a place or seat of authority and dominion.

Daniel 7:9
[9] *I beheld till the thrones were cast down, and the Ancient of days did sit, whose garment was white as snow, and the hair of his head like the pure wool: his throne was like the fiery flame, and his wheels as burning fire.*

The Throne was like a fiery flame. Fire speaks of judgment. So the saints will judge the world, and we shall also judge angels alike.

I Corinthians 6:2-3
² Do ye not know that the saints shall judge the world? and if the world shall be judged by you, are ye unworthy to judge the smallest matters?
³ Know ye not that we shall judge angels? how much more things that pertain to this life?

This judgment will not come out of our own authority or power, but it will come after we have been caught up to His throne or authority.

Isaiah 28:6
⁶ And for a spirit of judgment to him that sitteth in judgment, and for strength to them that turn the battle to the gate.

He shall also be "For a spirit of judgment to him that sits in judgment, and for strength to them that turn the battle to the gate." The saints shall judge the world, but it shall be with His authority, and He shall be the spirit of judgment.

Chapter Seventeen
The Right Hand of God

Hebrews 8:1
¹ Now of the things which we have spoken this is the sum: We have such an high priest, who is set on the right hand of the throne of the Majesty in the heavens;

The first son of God, Adam, was by the flesh and carnal, but the firstborn Son of God was of the Spirit. Our High Priest, who is set on high at the right hand of the throne of the majesty in the heavens, is Jesus.

A throne speaks of established power and authority.

The Right Hand speaks of the one that is preferred above the other; the firstborn or the established authority.

So the Father God laid his right hand upon the head of Jesus and the left upon Adam and he blessed the seed of Jesus.

Hebrews 12:2
² Looking unto Jesus the author and finisher of our faith; who for the joy that was set before him endured the cross, despising the shame, and is set down at the right hand of the throne of God.

Jesus, the author and finisher of our faith, for the joy that was set before him, endured the cross and shame (Hebrews 12:2). He is now established as a high priest forever. Because He overcame, He is now the established authority and power that is preferred above the old order of the first son, Adam.

Acts 7:55
⁵⁵ But he, being full of the Holy Ghost, looked up stedfastly into heaven, and saw the glory of God, and Jesus standing on the right hand of God.

Hebrews said that Jesus is sitting down at the right hand, but in Acts it says that Jesus is standing on the right hand of God.

Hebrews speaks of Jesus sitting down because He has overcome and has been established as the final authority and power. Acts speaks of Jesus standing because He was being looked at by the saints, as the one who had overcome and is the final authority and power. He is sending a message "look unto me, I am the author and finisher of your faith. I stand. I am with you and will be with you even unto the end of the world."

Standing or sitting, it does not change who He is, but it does speak to us and tells of the pattern that we should follow. We want to be seated with Him at His throne, but we must first stand, and work out our own salvation with fear and trembling (Philippians 2:12).

Romans 8:34
³⁴ Who is he that condemneth? It is Christ that died, yea rather, that is risen again, who is even at the right hand of God, who also maketh intercession for us.

The book of Romans speaks of Jesus being at the right hand of God with no mention of Him standing or sitting but making intercession for us.

Intercession
Pleading on behalf of another; to come between, in the sense of a barrier or an obstacle; to make a remark or to pose a question in the midst of a conversation; to bring influence or to take action on behalf of a person.

Jesus is acting on our behalf, and in the midst of judgment, He is representing us, pleading for us, and creating barriers that will save us. He is also bringing influence that will change us.

Hebrews 1:3
³ *Who being the brightness of his glory, and the express image of his person, and upholding all things by the word of his power, when he had by himself purged our sins, sat down on the right hand of the Majesty on high:*

Hebrews 10:12
¹² *But this man, after he had offered one sacrifice for sins forever, sat down on the right hand of God;*

I Peter 3:22
²² *Who is gone into heaven, and is on the right hand of God; angels and authorities and powers being made subject unto him.*

It is clearly expressed that Jesus is in that place of complete dominion over all powers. He has all authority in heaven and in earth.

Matthew 28:18
¹⁸ *And Jesus came and spake unto them, saying, All power is given unto me in heaven and in earth.*

Luke 22:69
⁶⁹ *Hereafter shall the Son of man sit on the right hand of the power of God.*

His expression of sitting is to show his permanent residence and established authority.

To sit on the right hand is the greatest power and authority available.

Genesis 48:13-20
¹³ *And Joseph took them both, Ephraim in his right hand toward Israel's left hand, and Manasseh in his left hand toward Israel's right hand, and brought them near unto him.*
¹⁴ *And Israel stretched out his right hand, and laid it upon Ephraim's head, who was the younger, and his left hand upon Manasseh's head, guiding his hands wittingly; for Manasseh was the firstborn.*

15 And he blessed Joseph, and said, God, before whom my father's Abraham and Isaac did walk, the God which fed me all my life long unto this day,
16 The Angel which redeemed me from all evil, bless the lads; and let my name be named on them, and the name of my father's Abraham and Isaac; and let them grow into a multitude in the midst of the earth.
17 And when Joseph saw that his father laid his right hand upon the head of Ephraim, it displeased him: and he held up his father's hand, to remove it from Ephraim's head unto Manasseh's head.
18 And Joseph said unto his father, Not so, my father: for this is the firstborn; put thy right hand upon his head.
19 And his father refused, and said, I know it, my son, I know it: he also shall become a people, and he also shall be great: but truly his younger brother shall be greater than he, and his seed shall become a multitude of nations.
20 And he blessed them that day, saying, In thee shall Israel bless, saying, God make thee as Ephraim and as Manasseh: and he set Ephraim before Manasseh.

Here is a picture of Israel wanting to bless the seed of His seed. The first was Adamic, carnal, earthly, sensual, and devilish; the second, Spirit-filled, holy, and true. God, the Father, is stretching forth his hand to pronounce blessings upon the firstborn.

In this instance the firstborn was chosen not after the flesh, but after the spirit; not chosen because of outward appearance but because of inward transformation. The one new man is in Christ, the man-child, the Jesus man.

Chapter Eighteen
The Son of Man

Ephesians 4:13
13 Till we all come in the unity of the faith, and of the knowledge of the Son of God, unto a perfect man, unto the measure of the stature of the fullness of Christ:

Jesus spoke of the day that is coming, when the Son of man would have the authority, power, and dominion of God Himself.

The Son of man is a perfect man—one who has come to the measure, stature and fullness of Christ—with Jesus being the head and the overcomers being the body with many members. This perfect man is not Jesus alone, but a complete body, the body of Jesus Christ.

Jesus certainly qualifies for all that is said about this Son of man, for He is the divine Head of this man, called "a perfect man." But it's not Jesus alone.

The Son of Man consists of a head and a body, the head is Jesus and the Body is His Christ, or body of many members.

Ephesians 4:13 (Amplified Bible)
13 [That it might develop] until we all attain oneness in the faith and in the comprehension of the [full and accurate] knowledge of the Son of God, that [we might arrive] at really mature manhood (the completeness of personality which is nothing less than the standard height of Christ's own perfection), the measure of the stature of the fullness of the Christ and the completeness found in Him.

It is Jesus and His body, joined together in the fullness of this Son of man, that fulfills all the scriptures concerning Him.

Genesis 1:26-27
*²⁶ And God said, Let us make man in our image, after our likeness: and l
et them have dominion over the fish of the sea, and over the fowl
of the air, and over the cattle, and over all the earth, and over
every creeping thing that creepeth upon the earth.
²⁷ So God created man in his own image, in the image of God created he
him; male and female created he them.*

And God said, "Let us make man in our image, after our likeness: and LET THEM HAVE DOMINION over the fish of the sea, and over the fowl of the air and over the cattle and over ALL THE EARTH, and over every creeping thing upon the earth. So God created man in His own image, in the image of God created He him; male and female created He them."

God's purpose in the beginning was for man to have dominion. He created him for this purpose. It looked as though Adam fell and lost this estate and dominion, but Jesus has come to restore it and more.

Luke 3:38
*³⁸ Which was the son of Enos, which was the son of Seth, which was the
son of Adam, which was the son of God.*

Adam was the son of God. If he did not sin, God's ultimate plan to make a perfect man would not have fulfilled. Though Adam had dominion over the earth, he was of the earth, and could only bring forth seed which would bear the image of the earthly. God had a higher plan and purpose for him.

I Corinthians 15:45
*⁴⁵ And so it is written, The first man Adam was made a living soul; the
last Adam was made a quickening spirit.*

The first Adam was made a LIVING SOUL but God wanted something more for His Son. The Word was made flesh and dwelt among us, suffered, and died, so that the last Adam could be a LIFE-GIVING SPIRIT! The Son of man is to have dominion over all the creation of God, but on a much higher plane than the first Adam ever had. This is our inheritance because of Jesus. The first Adam was made in the image and likeness of God but he was not one with him.

A true son comes from the loins of his Father. God did not make a perfect man in Genesis, but a carnal man with the ability to become perfect through divine processing. God knew that Adam would sin, so He already had a plan of redemption before Adam was created. The Gospel of John says that "in the beginning was the Word and the Word was with God and the Word was God, all things were made by him and without him was not anything made that was made" (John 1).

John 1:1-3
1 In the beginning was the Word, and the Word was with God, and the Word was God.
²The same was in the beginning with God.
³ All things were made by him; and without him was not any thing made that was made.

Jesus was in the beginning with God because He was God. God predetermined that He would make a perfect man who would become one with Him and share in His glory and power and rule the nations with Him, with a rod of iron.

Chapter Nineteen
What is Man?

Psalms 8:3-8
³ When I consider thy heavens, the work of thy fingers, the moon and the stars, which thou hast ordained;
⁴ What is man, that thou art mindful of him? and the son of man, that thou visitest him?
⁵ For thou hast made him a little lower than the angels, and hast crowned him with glory and honour.
⁶ Thou madest him to have dominion over the works of thy hands; thou hast put all things under his feet:
⁷ All sheep and oxen, yea, and the beasts of the field;
⁸ The fowl of the air, and the fish of the sea, and whatsoever passeth through the paths of the seas.

Psalms 8:3-8 (Amplified Bible)
³ When I view and consider Your heavens, the work of Your fingers, the moon and the stars, which You have ordained and established,
⁴ What is man that You are mindful of him, and the son of [earthborn] man that You care for him?
⁵ Yet You have made him but a little lower than God [or heavenly beings], and You have crowned him with glory and honor.
⁶ You made him to have dominion over the works of Your hands; You have put all things under his feet:
⁷ All sheep and oxen, yes, and the beasts of the field,
⁸ The birds of the air, and the fish of the sea, and whatever passes along the paths of the seas.

What is man? That you consider him above all of your creation, you gave him power and authority. The difference between man and beast is "he was made to be like God." Man was given glory and honor and made a little lower than the angels, but will one day judge angels.

Hebrews 2:5-9
⁵ For unto the angels hath he not put in subjection the world to come, whereof we speak.

⁶ But one in a certain place testified, saying, What is man, that thou art mindful of him? or the son of man that thou visitest him?
⁷ Thou madest him a little lower than the angels; thou crownedst him with glory and honour, and didst set him over the works of thy hands:
⁸ Thou hast put all things in subjection under his feet. For in that he put all in subjection under him, he left nothing that is not put under him. But now we see not yet all things put under him.
⁹ But we see Jesus, who was made a little lower than the angels for the suffering of death, crowned with glory and honour; that he by the grace of God should taste death for every man.

Hebrews 2:5-9 (Amplified Bible)
⁵ For it was not to angels that God subjected the habitable world of the future, of which we are speaking.
⁶ It has been solemnly and earnestly said in a certain place, What is man that You are mindful of him, or the son of man that You graciously and helpfully care for and visit and look after him?
⁷ For some little time You have ranked him lower than an inferior to the angels; You have crowned him with glory and honor and set him over the works of Your hands,
⁸ For You have put everything in subjection under his feet. Now in putting everything in subjection to man, He left nothing outside [of man's] control. But at present we do not yet see all things subjected to him [man].
⁹ But we are able to see Jesus, Who was ranked lower than the angels for a little while, crowned with glory and honor because of His having suffered death, in order that by the grace (unmerited favor) of God [to us sinners] He might experience death for every individual person.

Jesus tasted of death and conquered it because death found nothing of himself in Jesus that could have held him down. This gave Jesus the right and authority to take the keys of death and hell. Our destiny was then placed in the hands that hold the keys of death and hell. Our final condition will be determined by the one who holds the keys: "Jesus."

He left nothing that is not put under him (Son of man). But NOW we see NOT YET all things put under him (Son of man).

BUT WE SEE JESUS (Head of the Son of man corporate body), who WAS made a little lower than the angels for the suffering of death, CROWNED WITH GLORY AND HONOR. Jesus is bringing MANY SONS unto glory that He and they will be one, because He is not ashamed to call them brethren.

Many of us have not yet tapped into to the revelation of the Son of man; that Son of man spoken of is a man with a head and a body. The head of that son of man is Jesus and the body of the son of man is the many-membered body of Christ. The head, "Jesus," has already been perfected and the body which is the church is in the process of being perfected.

Judicially we have been made perfect because He is perfect, but in our experience we are not there yet. Though he is a male child with the ability to produce seed, he will not be able to produce seed until he grows up and becomes matured. Galatians 4:1 says, "[...] the heir. As long as he is a child, differeth nothing from a servant, though he be Lord of all."

Galatians 4:1
4 Now I say, That the heir, as long as he is a child, differeth nothing from a servant, though he be lord of all;

Jesus was born in a manger and when his life was threatened; his parents (tutors and governors) took him and fled the city, though He was the King of Kings and Lord of Lords and the Almighty One. When He became a man, He was made subject to the laws that He himself had put into place and could not break it to bring gain to the flesh. The body of Christ is in dire need to grow up and become like the head, "Jesus."

In the physical, our bodies need the nutrition of food, water, and sunlight to grow and to be sustained. Man has three stages in life. The number 3 speaks of completion for God is making a complete man who will become as He is.

1. Child

2. Boy
3. Man

Jesus did not begin his ministry until after He went down to the Jordan when He was about the age of 30. He was baptized and the heavens opened and He was declared to be called a man. The number 30 speaks of maturity. This is the 100 fold.

At the temple when He was about 12 years of age, He remained in the temple and took up the scroll and began to read "the spirit of the Lord is upon me" (Luke 4:18).

This represents the 60 fold and Pentecost, the baptism of the Holy Ghost. The number 12 speaks of divine government. In the manger he was but a child, the 30 fold. The son of man is made up of a head and a body and that body which is the temple and tabernacle, and the kingdom of God needs to be sanctified and become matured, one with the head.

Chapter Twenty
Sons Subject to the Father

Many of our traditional churches today have been teaching fantasies and old wives tales, especially us Pentecostals. Many of us have become superstitious and too emotional. I saw this one lady dancing in the spirit a couple years ago and her wig fell to the ground. She put a hold on the spirit, bent down and picked up the wig, put it back on her head and got right back to dancing in the spirit.

We have become so self-conscious about how we look and how we articulate our words. We consider the psychological side of our message more than the spiritual aspect of the Word. The Bible tells me that, no man comes unto God unless the spirit of God draws him. If we have to use psychology to keep people in church, it's not worth it. God is establishing His Kingdom here on the earth for us to declare Him.

A kingdom that is full of the King can only express the King. We are the body of Christ and members in particular; we are heirs and joint heirs with Christ. We are the brethren of Jesus, we are the body and Jesus is the head. The Kingdom of God is within us and we are the tabernacle of God. We are the Ark upon which the glory will rest. Jesus is the Ark of safety and we are the Ark that will bear his glory. We are the latter house that was spoken of, where it says that the glory of the latter will be greater than the former.

I recently saw the movie *Ice Age*. One of the mammoths grew up with two opossums and was taught to believe that she was an opossum just like the other two. One day she came upon another mammoth who knew that he was a mammoth. She was so convinced, though, that she was a mammoth that she even introduced herself as an opossum.

There is an identity crisis in the church today. So many of us don't know who we are and why we are here. With no sense of purpose, we allow others to tell us who we are and what we should be. I want to declare to all of us today that we are children of the King; our Father is the King of the earth. We are intended to become one with God.

We live in a fantasy world and it is much easier for people to conform to what they see, but what they see may not necessarily be what they should conform to.

The things to which God wants us to conform are seen through the eye of the Spirit. The spirit realm dictates the physical realm. The mind or soul dictates the actions and behavior of the body or the flesh.

The things of the spirit must be spiritually discerned, because the flesh just cannot interpret the language of the spirit.

1 Corinthians 15:24-28
[24] *Then cometh the end, when he shall have delivered up the kingdom to God, even the Father; when he shall have put down all rule and all authority and power.*

Then the end comes when He shall deliver up the bride who was adorned for her husband as a chaste virgin. The overcomer, the man-child, the Lamb's wife, the brethren of Jesus, the Kingdom of God, the domain where God has all dominion and those who are governed by it shall have dominion over all things, having all things put under their feet. Thus, we are being made ambassadors and representatives of the King of Kings who is the King of this divine Kingdom.

[25]*For he must reign, till he hath put all enemies under his feet.*

All enemies, meaning the flesh and the works of the flesh, will be under total subjection of the son of man, and this son of man is a complete corporate man: Jesus being the head and the church being the Body.

²⁶ The last enemy that shall be destroyed is death.

The last enemy is death and we as the body of Christ have not yet come to the full adoption of sons. We have not yet been perfected, but Jesus was. We are still in the process, but the day is coming when we shall be transformed in the twinkling of an eye and become one with Him just as He and the Father are one. The #1 representing God.

²⁷ For he hath put all things under his feet. But when he saith all things are put under him, it is manifest that he is excepted, which did put all things under him.
²⁸ And when all things shall be subdued unto him, then shall the Son also himself be subject unto him that put all things under him, that God may be all in all.

The ultimate purpose is for God to sit on the throne of His Kingdom. To suggest that one will sit means that there will be some sort of comfort level and the place will be a place of rest. If all of God could come in us, we would become one with Him, and, if the flesh fails to dominate and the spirit regains dominion, we will become one with the spirit.

The greatest compliment that we could give the Father is to grow up and become like Him.

If God can find rest in us, it would mean that we have found rest in Him. He is our ultimate resting place, meaning that there will be no more efforts of justification or redemption. This means that we would have been fully justified and redeemed and have come to the place of perfection. Perfection does not need work nor does it need refining, that which could have been shaken was shaken and all that is left is the final product, a perfect man.

1 Corinthians 15:24-25 (Amplified Bible)
²⁴ After that comes the end (the completion), when He delivers over the kingdom to God the Father after rendering inoperative and abolishing every [other] rule and every authority and power.
²⁵ For [Christ] must be King and reign until He has put all [His] enemies under His feet.

The enemy is the flesh and the works of the flesh, all carnality. It started with the serpent in the garden and was passed on to Eve, who passed it on the Adam, who passed it on to us. The book of Romans says that all have sinned and come short of the glory of God. A little leaven spoils the whole lump.

1 Corinthians 15:26-28 (Amplified Bible)
²⁶ The last enemy to be subdued and abolished is death.
²⁷ For He [the Father] has put all things in subjection under His [Christ's] feet. But when it says, All things are put in subjection [under Him], it is evident that He [Himself] is excepted Who does the subjecting of all things to Him.
²⁸ However, when everything is subjected to Him, then the Son Himself will also subject Himself to [the Father] Who put all things under Him, so that God may be all in all [be everything to everyone, supreme, the indwelling and controlling factor of life] When everything is made subject to the Son, then he will be made subject to the Father.

God's plan is to be everything to everyone, but this can only happen when everyone makes Him everything to them. We need to begin to lose some things to make room for everything, bearing in mind that God is a big God and He owns heaven and earth; in fact, all things belongs to him.

Jesus will forever be the Head of this corporate body. They will never operate independent of God. Of this body Jesus said: "I will be his God, and he shall be my Son."

Revelation 21:17
¹⁷ And he measured the wall thereof, an hundred and forty and four cubits, according to the measure of a man, that is, of the angel.

Revelation 21:17 (Amplified Bible)
¹⁷ He measured its wall also 144 cubits (about 72 yards) by a man's measure [of a cubit from his elbow to his third fingertip], which is [the measure] of the angel.

6x12=72
72 Yards = 144 cubits
12x12=144
72x2=144

2 represents a testimony.
6 represents the number of man.
12 represents divine government or God's Government.

72 represents man who is coming into divine government through a testimony.
144 represents perfect divine government.
It does not speak of a physical quantity but it represents a people who have been perfected and have become one with God's divine order.

 This body of Sons will never be equal to or have dominion over God, their Father. This Son Company will forever be subject to the headship of Jesus, that God may be all in all.

 Jesus does not occupy second place in the Kingdom of God, for there is no one ABOVE HIM. He has been exalted to the place above ALL principalities and power and might, and dominion, and EVERY name that is named both in this world and the world to come. His name is above EVERY name. No name above His.

 The many sons that are coming to Glory are a bit different. Though we will become one in nature and character, we will always be subject to Him. The sons will act in the authority of the Father, but the Father will always be the Father and the son will always be the son, subject to the Father.

Chapter Twenty One
The Mark for the Prize Part One

2 Corinthians 11:24
[24] *Of the Jews five times received I forty stripes save one.*

THE STRIPING OF PAUL

The #5 speaks of Favor, Grace and the five-fold ministry.

Strong's H2568 – *chamesh* חָמֵשׁ khä·māsh'

CHET:
    The 8th letter of the Hebrew alphabet that speaks of a fence, enclosure = inner room; heart; private; separate.
The #8 speaks of a new beginning.

    The #4 speaks of the world and all that is carnal (flesh). Adam being the first man started off as a man who was created out of the carnal dust of the ground. A second man, who was Jesus, came into the picture in the form of God in the flesh (carnal), although He was not of a carnal bloodline. A second #4 was added to the picture of God so #4+#4 = 8.

    In other words, Adam was never going to be able to give his sons a chance of perfection; but, Jesus through the Spirit created a way that was predestinated by God to bring many sons to glory.

THE LAMB OF GOD, PERFECT SACRIFICE

Genesis 22:1-2
[1] *And it came to pass after these things, that God did tempt Abraham, and said unto him, Abraham: and he said, Behold, here I am.*
[2] *And he said, Take now thy son, thine only son Isaac, whom thou lovest, and get thee into the land of Moriah; and offer him there for a*

burnt offering upon one of the mountains which I will tell thee of.

Moriah:

Strong's H4179 – *Mowriyah* מוֹרִיָּה mō·rē·yä'
Moriah = "chosen by Jehovah"
1) the place where Abraham took Isaac for sacrifice
2) the mount on the eastern edge of Jerusalem on which Solomon built the temple

The Lamb of God, the perfect sacrifice, the ultimate sacrifice was chosen by God. The location of the sacrifice was also chosen by God. Furthermore, God himself provided the sacrifice.

Abraham had faith in His God knowing that His God was so real that He was prepared to obey God even if He had to give His only son. Notice that He said something that was so profound, "God will provide for Himself a sacrifice".

Genesis 22:8
⁸ And Abraham said, My son, God will provide himself a lamb for a burnt offering: so they went both of them together.

Genesis 22:13
¹³ And Abraham lifted up his eyes, and looked, and behold behind him a ram caught in a thicket by his horns: and Abraham went and took the ram, and offered him up for a burnt offering in the stead of his son.

This chosen place was God's designation. God's ultimate plan was without error and He knew exactly what Abraham was going to do. So in the middle of His request to Abraham, He provided the sacrifice that was worthy of saving the life of Isaac. This ram was a male; his horn was his glory, as "horn" speaks of power. To say this another way, He who had the power to lay down His life and take it back up, positioned Himself in the thicket of mortal flesh so that He could redeem the sons of promise. Though He had all the power to set himself free, He chose to suffer the fate of the cross and endure the bruising for you and me so that we would be granted access to the Father as sons and heirs to His Kingdom.

Revelations 5:6
6 And I beheld, and, lo, in the midst of the throne and of the four beasts, and in the midst of the elders, stood a Lamb as it had been slain, having seven horns and seven eyes, which are the seven Spirits of God sent forth into all the earth.

Bless God! Here is where it all took place: in the midst of the throne of the four beasts, in the midst of the elders. The Lamb stood as it had been slain, but He had seven horns. The #7 speaks of perfection and the horns speak of power; the seven eyes, of the all-seeing God; the seven spirits are the spirit of perfection that is one and the same "the spirit of God." "Into all the earth" means this earthly body that we are in is being filled with all of God.

Another way of saying this is that we are becoming one with Jesus, just as He and the Father are one. So ultimately, God is bringing us into a place of maturity where we can take our place as full grown sons who will become a pillar in the temple of God, who will become one with the Lamb, and who will be filled will all of God. The seven eyes mean that we will have perfect eyes to see all truth for nothing shall be hid. Then, the seven horns mean that we will be walking with the full unlimited power of God to do the greater works as promised by Jesus. The throne of the four beasts is the throne of the sons who is gone on to perfection and has been transformed into one who carries the glory of God, a cherub.

Revelations 21:21-23
21 And the twelve gates were twelve pearls: every several gate was of one pearl: and the street of the city was pure gold, as it were transparent glass.
22 And I saw no temple therein: for the Lord God Almighty and the Lamb are the temple of it.
23 And the city had no need of the sun, neither of the moon, to shine in it: for the glory of God did lighten it, and the Lamb is the light thereof.

The #12 speaks of divine government. The twelve gates are the sons of God who have grown up into the divine government of God. The Pearl is very unique, as it is made with one grain of sand that makes its way into the eyes of the oyster. It grows with many layers and is transformed into a precious jewel. Several gates were layered into one pearl, so God is in the process of layering us who are the gates, into His divine order being formed into one pearl. The #1 speaks of God, so we who are many are being layered into one who is God.

We are the City of God and the Gold is representative of the Glory of God. Transparent glass means that it is totally clear, containing no darkness—all light and no shadows. The Lord God Almighty and the Lamb are one and the same, as are the temple or light of that City, who we are. No need of sun, because we are light bearers or light bringers. We have put on Christ have put on light, for God is light and in Him there is no darkness. No darkness means that there are no more shadows. The Glory of God and the Lamb became the light of the City. When we have put on the mind of Christ we have been transformed or transfigured into a glorified son in the express image of God.

Revelations 22:1-4
¹ And he shewed me a pure river of water of life, clear as crystal, proceeding out of the throne of God and of the Lamb.
² In the midst of the street of it, and on either side of the river, was there the tree of life, which bare twelve manner of fruits, and yielded her fruit every month: and the leaves of the tree were for the healing of the nations.
³ And there shall be no more curse: but the throne of God and of the Lamb shall be in it; and his servants shall serve him:
⁴ And they shall see his face; and his name shall be in their foreheads.

John said "he showed me" a pure river of water of life. Pure expresses that the water is not contaminated, the water here is significant of the word, clear as crystal, meaning that it was transparent, without defects, could be clearly seen. This water came gushing out from the throne of God and from the Lamb which is one and the same. In other words, it was a pure word that came forth from God.

In the midst of the street, and on both sides of the river, to the left and to the right, was the tree of life, who is Jesus and His leaves or His offspring was for the healing of the nations. See the many sons of God bringing healing to the nations. To get to the Source we must be connected and when we are connected to the Source, anything that connects with us will also get connected to the same source. This tree bares twelve manners of fruit. The #12 speaks of divine government, so this tree of life, who is Jesus, distributed His fruits of divine government to His many sons. The fruits were distributed every month, twelve months in a year, according to the order of God.

The throne of God and the Lamb are in this city and all His servants were serving Him with willing hearts. A son, as long as he is a child is no different from a servant so the servant and the son are one and the same. These sons have come to a place where they can see the face of God and live for His name. His nature shall be "IN" their foreheads. See, to have the nature of God in your forehead is to have put on the mind of Christ, so we would have put on the mind of Christ.

A WALL OR FENCE

Revelation 21:16-18
[16] *And the city lieth foursquare, and the length is as large as the breadth: and he measured the city with the reed, twelve thousand furlongs. The length and the breadth and the height of it are equal.*
[17] *And he measured the wall thereof, an hundred and forty and four cubits, according to the measure of a man, that is, of the angel.*
[18] *And the building of the wall of it was of jasper: and the city was pure gold, like unto clear glass.*

Here, we see a wall that fenced the City of God on all four sides. This city had all equal measurements in length, breadth, and height. It measured twelve thousand furlongs and the wall, a hundred and forty four cubits, according to the measure of a man.

That wall is none other than the wall of God's holy temple. You and I are temples of the living God. So when He talks about the wall being equal, He is talking about us becoming one with our Father.

The #1,000 speaks of divine completeness and the Glory of the Father. When you multiply divine completeness with divine order you get complete divine order, full of glory.

The #144 speaks of complete divine order. Because the #12 speaks of divine order, so out of 12 x 12 =144 will come order.

One cubit is 18 inches and 144 is the result of 12 x 12, so what has happened is that the divine order of God has consumed the spirit of anti-Christ that was rampant within the heart of man and brought him into His divine government.

The #18 speaks of Anti-Christ, or anything that is in opposition of God. See, the #18 was a result of the # 6 + 6 + 6 = 18 and the #6 is represented and speaks of man for he was created on the 6th day. Also, #6 x 3 = 18

The # 3 speaks of completion for God is complete in the Godhead of the Father, the Son and the Holy Spirit.

That City spoken of in verse 18 is the City of God, the Temple of God, the People of God, and the Tabernacle of God. He said that this same City was pure Gold. Gold speaks of the Glory of God, so He is bringing us into a place where He can fill us with all of Himself so when the world sees us they will see Christ in us, the hope of Glory. Clear as glass, in anticipation of knowing Him, we now see through a glass darkly, but we are coming to a place where we will see Him face to face and live.

1 Corinthians 13:12
¹² *For now we see through a glass, darkly; but then face to face: now I know in part; but then shall I know even as also I am known.*

Four major things happened here, speaking of the present and the future, the now and the then, in respect to where we are today and where we will be when we have grown up into Him in all things.

Now

    For now we see through a glass darkly
    Now I know in part

Now, suggesting that we are in the present tense and our wilderness experience is not yet over. We are at the juncture of seeing through a glass darkly. Suggesting that we are able to see, but our vision is somewhat blurred. It requires extra effort, extra determination and focus. This glass or this dark glass suggests that a shadow is present and a shadow can only be cast using light. So as the light of the Son of God is shining upon us we are beginning to see that which is revealed by the light.

A caution to all of us while we are looking through this glass: some of the figures that are seen may not necessarily be totally clear to our comprehension because of the darkness. This shadow or darkness serves as a buffer between God and man. Some of the time we get ahead of ourselves, and can get hurt, even destroy ourselves given too much at one time. Not only can it destroy us, but also those around us if we are not guided by God's divine order. We know in part because of the darkness. Only when the darkness is totally removed or exposed by the light will we be able to see as He sees and to know as He knows.

Romans 8:1-2
¹ *There is therefore now no condemnation to them which are in Christ Jesus, who walk not after the flesh, but after the Spirit.*
² *For the law of the Spirit of life in Christ Jesus hath made me free from the law of sin and death.*

In the now, here in the present, today, there is therefore, NO condemnation to them which are in Christ. What a revelation to us as sons and daughters of God. When we come before the Father after we have been born again and begin to ask His forgiveness for the sins of yesterday and that of our forefathers, His response is "what sin?" See, you can only be condemned if you are guilty of sin.

But thank God that we are no longer guilty of sin because Jesus took our sin upon His own body so that He would be condemned in our place.

Then
> But then face to face
> But then shall I know even as I am known

Then suggest the future or things to come, something that has not yet happened to us, an experience that we have not yet encountered.

1 John 3:2
² Beloved, now are we the sons of God, and it doth not yet appear what we shall be: but we know that, when he shall appear, we shall be like him; for we shall see him as he is.

When a day that shall be, "then" the word that tells us that we have a hope, and that hope is to be transformed and become just like Him. We shall see Him in all His fullness because we will be just like Him, for we will become one with Him.

THE VEIL OF THE TABERNACLE

Matthew 27:50-51
⁵⁰ Jesus, when he had cried again with a loud voice, yielded up the ghost.
⁵¹ And, behold, the veil of the temple was rent in twain from the top to the bottom; and the earth did quake, and the rocks rent;

Hebrews 10:16-20
¹⁶ This is the covenant that I will make with them after those days, saith the Lord, I will put my laws into their hearts, and in their minds will I write them;
¹⁷ And their sins and iniquities will I remember no more.
¹⁸ Now where remission of these is, there is no more offering for sin.
¹⁹ Having therefore, brethren, boldness to enter into the holiest by the blood of Jesus,
²⁰ By a new and living way, which he hath consecrated for us, through the veil, that is to say, his flesh;

The Hebrew letter "Chet" speaks of a wall, fence, or a veil of separation.

The veil served as a protection to the people of God. When we look at Jesus as the son of God we see "God" hiding in the body of a man. He contained himself within the body of a man and limited himself to the laws and principles that He himself has set for man to abide by.

The idea was not to alienate himself from man, but to make himself approachable and accessible, allowing man to relate to what He knows. Just as there was a veil in the temple separating man from the full glory of God, that veil was not meant to protect God from man but to protect man from God. If man had only come into direct contact with the full glory he would surely die.

So when God came in the flesh, it served as a veil to protect man from the full glory of God. But there came a time when that veil of the temple was torn and rend in two. So was Jesus who was torn when he was beaten with forty stripes save one. Just as the veil was rend into two, the #2 speaks of a testimony and Jesus came here to testify of His Father and His great love for us.

Chapter Twenty Two
The Mark for the Prize, Part Two

2 Corinthians 11:24
[24] *Of the Jews five times received I forty stripes save one.*

THE STRIPING OF PAUL

The #5 speaks of Favor, Grace and the five-fold ministry.

Strong's H2568 – *chamesh* חָמֵשׁ khä·mäsh'

MEM:
The 13th letter of the Hebrew alphabet that speaks of water, what flows down = immensity, or chaos.

The #40 which speaks of trial and probation.
The #40 is a result of the #4 x #10 which is = 40.

All that is carnal, fleshly and worldly has been multiplied 10 times. The #10 speaks of testing and the law. All that is worldly, fleshly and carnal must be tested by the law or the standards and principles of God.

THE TEN COMMANDMENTS

Law
Established standards and principles codified and enforced by a governing authority for its constituencies.

Strong's H8451 – *towrah* תּוֹרָה tō·rä'
The Law speaks of direction, direction, instruction, a body of legal directives.

TAV:
The 22nd letter of the Hebrew Alphabet which speaks of a sign, signature, mark, a cross, the sealing of a covenant.
Represented by the #400 which speaks of a period of time that is perfect.

VAV:
The 6th letter of the Hebrew Alphabet which speaks of a nail, a hook, that which is used to fasten, join together, secure, and add.
Represented by the #6 which speaks of man

RESH:
The 20th letter of the Hebrew Alphabet speaks of the head, leader, person, the one who is in the highest position of authority.
The #200 speaks of insufficiency.

HEY:
The 5th letter of the Hebrew Alphabet speaks of a window, to behold, to reveal divine inspiration, that which comes through favor.
The #5 speaks of Grace and the five-fold ministry.

This "Torah" or Law was implemented and put in place to place limits upon man, to keep him in line with the principles of the one who wrote the Law.

The #22 speaks of sonship or the sons of light. God, through His divine purpose, has superimposed His son in the form of a carnal man to create a new covenant and set a seal of redemption upon His sons that will bring them into a place where time is unlimited. Through the nailing and fastening of the Son of God to the Cross, He was able to secure our salvation and make us part of His eternal Kingdom, though we were destined for death being carnal.

The #20 speaks of the blood and we know that Jesus shed his blood upon the Cross for you and me. So He who is the head of all things, even Christ, has showed His righteousness to the Father in our place, because our righteousness is as filthy rags and has deemed us insufficient and unworthy and unable to redeem ourselves. By the Grace of God toward us, however, we are now accepted in the beloved.

Genesis 2:17
[17] But of the tree of the knowledge of good and evil, thou shalt not eat of it: for in the day that thou eatest thereof thou shalt surely die.

Genesis 3:9-11
[9] And the LORD God called unto Adam, and said unto him, Where art thou?
[10] And he said, I heard thy voice in the garden, and I was afraid, because I was naked; and I hid myself.
[11] And he said, Who told thee that thou wast naked? Hast thou eaten of the tree, whereof I commanded thee that thou shouldest not eat?

Genesis 3:17
[17] And unto Adam he said, Because thou hast hearkened unto the voice of thy wife, and hast eaten of the tree, of which I commanded thee, saying, Thou shalt not eat of it: cursed is the ground for thy sake; in sorrow shalt thou eat of it all the days of thy life;

Romans 8:20
[20] For the creature was made subject to vanity, not willingly, but by reason of him who hath subjected the same in hope,

The Law was first given to Adam and to Eve in the Garden of Eden with a hope in the mind of God, knowing that man would eventually sin. In preparation for what was about to take place, God had to place divine limit upon His own creation for a great purpose. God had to place divine limit upon man, knowing that man was insufficient of saving Himself should he fail because he was created out of the dust of the ground as a carnal being and became a living soul. So looking very closely at the plan of God, He incorporated the Law.

#22 speaks of sonship and the sons of light and we know that God is light so if we are the sons of light then we are also the sons of God.

#400 speaks of a perfect period of time and we also know that God is bringing us into a place where we will live and reign with him forever.

#6 speaks of man and his carnal Adamic nature and character, the carnal side of man.

#20 speaks of the blood and we know that in order for man to ever get back to God he would have to be redeemed and we also know that it is only the blood of Jesus that is able to remit sin and redeem man back to God.

#200 speaks of the insufficiency of man because man was unable to save himself.

#5 speaks of Grace and the divine favor of God that would be made available to man and would not require any physical work on the behalf of man.

We are now able to see that God is the one who subjected Adam to hope, not with the help of Adam, but with a greater purpose in mind. It was all God's doing when he imposed the Law upon man. So this creature, Adam, was made to subject himself to the characteristics of the carnal mind, not at his own will but at the will of his creator. God knew that Adam was the beginning of His creation and not the final product of a man in the express image of Himself.

Romans 4:13
[13] *For the promise, that he should be the heir of the world, was not to Abraham, or to his seed, through the law, but through the righteousness of faith.*

The Law was put into motion by God, but man broke the Law. Because of the principles set forth, man was judged. And because of man's rebellion, God had to intervene and set faith in motion to bring about constant change from one generation to another.

Romans 5:20
[20] *Moreover the law entered, that the offence might abound. But where sin abounded, grace did much more abound:*

Romans 8:2
[2] *For the law of the Spirit of life in Christ Jesus hath made me free from the law of sin and death.*

Romans 8:4
[4] *That the righteousness of the law might be fulfilled in us, who walk not after the flesh, but after the Spirit.*

Galatians 2:19
[19] *For I through the law am dead to the law, that I might live unto God.*

The 13th Son

The #13 speaks of Jesus being the 13th Son which is also representative of the sons of Jesus that were to come out of Jesus. The #13 is a result of #10 + #3

Through the Law and the test, God implemented his plan of completion to bring His many sons to glory.

NOAH'S ARK

Genesis 5:32
[32] *And Noah was five hundred years old: and Noah begat Shem, Ham, and Japheth.*

Genesis 6:8
[8] *But Noah found grace in the eyes of the L*ORD.

Looking at the principle of Grace represented by the #5 and the #3 which is represented by the three sons of Noah, we can clearly see Shem, Ham, and Japheth as a product of Grace, or the sons of Grace. Noah being just like Jesus, who in essence is Grace Himself, is bringing forth many sons that will be full of the Godhead (the Father, the Son and the Holy Spirit); so we are the sons of Grace, the sons of Jesus.

Genesis 7:6
⁶ And Noah was six hundred years old when the flood of waters was upon the earth.

Genesis 8:6
⁶ And it came to pass at the end of forty days, that Noah opened the window of the ark which he had made:

The #6 represents the flesh and the #40 speaks of testing and the Law as described above.

Genesis 6:3
³ And the LORD said, My spirit shall not always strive with man, for that he also is flesh: yet his days shall be an hundred and twenty years.

Acts 1:15
¹⁵ And in those days Peter stood up in the midst of the disciples, and said, (the number of names together were about an hundred and twenty,)

So God said that His Spirit shall not always strive with man because he is flesh. In order for the spirit of God to strive or live with man and in man, the flesh of man would have to die or be brought to an end.

So the #120 represents the end of all flesh. It took the flood waters, which represent the judgment of God, to bring an end to the carnal man. In the same manner, the Spirit of God at the upper room would bring an end to all flesh when the Spirit of God takes over. We are at our greatest strength when God takes over.

Chapter Twenty Three
The Mark for the Prize, Part Three

2 Corinthians 11:24
²⁴ Of the Jews five times received I forty stripes save one.

THE STRIPING OF PAUL

The #5 speaks of Favor, Grace and the five-fold ministry.

Strong's H2568 – *chamesh* חָמֵשׁ khä·mäsh'

SHIN:
The 21ˢᵗ letter of the Hebrew alphabet which speaks of teeth = to consume, devour, and destroy.

The #300 speaks of complete deliverance.
The #100 speaks of completeness, therefore #100 x #3 = #300.
The #3 speaks of completion, so completeness x completion is equal to complete deliverance.
The #21 speaks of complete perfection.
The #7 speaks of perfection, so #7 x #3 = perfection x completion.

Proverbs 30:14
¹⁴ There is a generation, whose teeth are as swords, and their jaw teeth as knives, to devour the poor from off the earth, and the needy from among men.

There is a generation whose mouth speaks sharp words, with their jaw teeth as sharp as knives that are set on devouring the "poor" from off the earth and the "needy" from among men. The words that we speak should be full of spirit and life—just like Jesus. In the beginning, God spoke the Word and the world and all that exists into existence. If we take our rightful place in the Kingdom of God, we should be speaking things into existence as though they were.

Amos 4:1
4 Hear this word, ye kine of Bashan, that are in the mountain of Samaria, which oppress the poor, which crush the needy, which say to their masters, Bring, and let us drink.

Deuteronomy 15:11
¹¹ For the poor shall never cease out of the land: therefore I command thee, saying, Thou shalt open thine hand wide unto thy brother, to thy poor, and to thy needy, in thy land.

POOR; Strong's H1803 - *dallah* דַּלָּה dal·lä'
Speaks of the poor (usually a group of helpless people)

Dalet
The 4th letter of the Hebrew Alphabet speaks of a door, an opening, an entry, or a pathway. It is represented by the #4 which speaks of all that is earthly and of material creation.

Lamed
The 12th letter of the Hebrew Alphabet speaks of divine Government and order.
It represents a goad, a staff, a symbol of authority and divine power. It is represented by the #30 which speaks of maturity and development.

Hey
The 5th letter of the Hebrew Alphabet, which speaks of Grace and divine Favor, represents a window or an entrance, to reveal, to bring inspiration. It is represented by the #5 which speaks of Grace and Favor.

Another word for "poor" is helpless. Another word for helplessness is insufficient. When we have come to realize our limitation, only then can we see the omnipotence of God Almighty. Only when we have come to realize our insufficiency can we see the Glory of the one true and living God. When we have come to the place of understanding that we are helpless, then we will understand the need for God and the need to allow him to be God.

Matthew 11:28-30
²⁸ Come unto me, all ye that labour and are heavy laden, and I will give you rest.
²⁹ Take my yoke upon you, and learn of me; for I am meek and lowly in heart: and ye shall find rest unto your souls.
³⁰ For my yoke is easy, and my burden is light.

Matthew 5:3
³ Blessed are the poor in spirit: for theirs is the kingdom of heaven.

To be poor simply means to have a need or a lack of something. When we are in lack we open ourselves up to having that need met. Having a need is an opportunity to encounter God through his divine provision and His ability to meet our need. But if we are not poor and have no lack, then we have no need of God. Say to God: "Here I am in need. Help me for I am weak and poor." We then say to Him, "I have realized my limitations and I need you to fill my lack and meet my need." To be poor in spirit is to say, "I need you God."

Galatians 3:27
²⁷ For as many of you as have been baptized into Christ have put on Christ

Being baptized into Christ is being born again, but being born again does not mean water baptism but the Baptism of Blood, and that of the blood of Jesus Christ. For it is only the blood of Christ that can remit sin.

Romans 13:14
¹⁴ But put ye on the Lord Jesus Christ, and make not provision for the flesh, to fulfill the lusts thereof.

There is a generation of sons that are being born in this due season. This man-child, who is not content to live in bondage and the weakness and poverty of the flesh, but desires to take hold of the promise of God and rise up and devour the carnal Adamic nature that is within us as with devouring teeth.

The poor will no longer be poor, but rich in Christ. There will be no lack or need because our provision is in Christ.

A door has been opened through Grace knowing that we are a carnal creation and limited in the flesh. Through His divine government He will bring us to maturity, however. Poverty and helplessness will be ripped away by the word of life as the new man rises up in Christ.

Galatians 5:15
[15] *But if ye bite and devour one another, take heed that ye be not consumed one of another.*

In this present time, we are asked to be mindful, not to use our words to destroy one another; for many have lost their way and have lost sight of the goal. Surely, the scriptures say, "the weapons of our warfare are not carnal, but mighty through God" (II Corinthians 10:4). Our brothers and sisters are not the enemy, but rather, Satan—the accuser of the brethren. So remain focused and fight the good fight against the flesh of our minds and love one another.

1 Peter 5:8
[8] *Be sober, be vigilant; because your adversary the devil, as a roaring lion, walketh about, seeking whom he may devour:*

Revelation 12:4
[4] *And his tail drew the third part of the stars of heaven, and did cast them to the earth: and the dragon stood before the woman which was ready to be delivered, for to devour her child as soon as it was born.*

The #39 speaks of disease in the feet.
The #39 is a result of #30 + #9 which was brought together for the purpose of bringing man to a place of maturity and fruitfulness.

The #30 is #3 x #10 = #30 as we saw above, the #10 represents testing and the Law and the #3 represents completion just as we know that the constitution of God consists of three major parts:

1. Father
2. Holy Spirit
3. Son

So, Jesus, being the son of God, came into this world as a mortal man to lead the way, knowing that He was the third member of the Godhead. He had to endure and abide by the very laws and principles that He Himself had imposed upon man. Jesus had to overcome and fulfill that law and the test of the law, so that he could grow up and become of age as a matured son before He could redeem man back unto Himself.

The #9 is a result of #3 x #3 = #9 which speaks of fruitfulness.
So completion x completion is equal to complete fruitfulness. God is bringing His body of many members to completion and fruitfulness.

THE MANGO TREE WITH RIPE FRUITS

As concerning the mango tree, I have somewhat observed the characteristics of the mango tree in the Island of Trinidad. There are several types of mangos that are grown on the Island of Trinidad and Tobago, but one in particular that is called the "Duduce." It is just about the most delicious mango you can ever bring your mouth in contact with. The tree does not grow more than about 30-40 feet in height, but for the most part they stay about 20 feet in height. Trinidad is part of the tropics in the Caribbean.

It is usually very hot when the sun comes in contact with the mangoes that are at the very end of the branches, which are usually hard to reach by the human hands. They look beautiful red and yellow with a little orange and it seems like they cry out for help, "come and get me." Mangos are a very strange fruit but when

Duduce meets the mouth, it is like a love affair that has been waiting to happen for centuries.

I will explain what typically happens in the Islands. There is no easy way to reach out and pick the mango, we would climb the trees most of the times but still were unable to reach the crying mangoes. So we would climb back down the tree and begin a search for small rocks and dry branches lying on the ground, of which we would use to pelt and throw at the crying mangoes in an effort to get it to fall to the ground so "mango can meet mouth."

Just to express what fun that experience was, we would usually climb the tree and eat as much as we could and climb down only after we were full. So in the process of pelting at the ripe crying mangoes, we would often hit bunches that were green and unwanted and they would fall to the ground with no spark of a love affair. We would pursue pelting until we got the one that we initially eyed and that would stop the beating on the mango tree.

Here is the moral of this beautiful love story: we pursue fruits that are ripe and juicy and ready to have an experience with us, but in the process of hungry harvesters, we sometimes inflict pain and cause hurt to the tree. We are the trees of God's garden. If we have fruit that is desired by others and in their effort to make contact with that fruit, they might sometimes cause us hurt because they want what we have.

So when you find that people are throwing dry wood and rocks at you, it just might be that they want the fruit that you possess. If people are not throwing stuff at you, maybe you need to check your fruit making sure you have been exposed to the Son. If your fruit is hidden, men will not seek after it. Saying you have the fruit of love and not showing it is not justice to the fruit.

When Jesus went up to the fig tree, He was looking for fruit and could not find any. When people come to you they should be able to find the fruits of the spirit that have been exposed to the Son of God looking ripe and enticing.

The #40 speaks of trial and probation. The #40 as expressed above tells of the test of our humanity and the work of salvation that God has brought to us. The wilderness is not a killer but an experience that will bring forth a testimony. Without the test, there will be no testimony.

The Husbandman is coming back to His garden hoping to find fruit that has been matured and ready for harvest. How is your fruit developing? Are people looking at you hoping to have some of your fruit because it stands out because of the exposure to the Son of God? Or is your fruit dormant? Submit yourselves therefore to God and to His ordinances that we may grow in His grace.

Chapter Twenty Four
Healing of the Feet

2 Corinthians 11:24
²⁴ Of the Jews five times received I forty stripes save one.

THE STRIPING OF PAUL

The #5 speaks of Favor, Grace and the five-fold ministry.

Strong's H2568 – *chamesh* חָמֵשׁ khä·mäsh'

Peter and John at the Gate Beautiful

Acts 3:1-9
¹ Now Peter and John went up together into the temple at the hour of prayer, being the ninth hour.
² And a certain man lame from his mother's womb was carried, whom they laid daily at the gate of the temple which is called Beautiful, to ask alms of them that entered into the temple;
³ Who seeing Peter and John about to go into the temple asked an alms.
⁴ And Peter, fastening his eyes upon him with John, said, Look on us.
⁵ And he gave heed unto them, expecting to receive something of them.
⁶ Then Peter said, Silver and gold have I none; but such as I have give I thee: In the name of Jesus Christ of Nazareth rise up and walk.
⁷ And he took him by the right hand, and lifted him up: and immediately his feet and ankle bones received strength.
⁸ And he leaping up stood, and walked, and entered with them into the temple, walking, and leaping, and praising God.
⁹ And all the people saw him walking and praising God:

THE LAME MAN AT THE GATE

According to the book of Acts, the man that was at the gate beautiful had been crippled for 39 years and was begging for alms. With no resolve or resolution to his disease in his feet, he did the only thing he knew how to do in order to stay alive. He did not know that he was royalty. He did not know that he was a king, a priest and a son. He did not know that he was an heir to the throne of God and that he had access to the Father and was worthy of the promise by faith.

A KING WHO DID NOT KNOW IT

This beggar man lame in the feet did not know that he was a King and that he was part of a Kingdom. He did not know that he had a right to the throne. He did not know that words were there for his commanding. He was like a sleeping giant who needed to wake up and realize that he was a giant.

Proverbs 25:2
² It is the glory of God to conceal a thing: but the honour of kings is to search out a matter.

1 Peter 2:9-10
⁹ But ye are a chosen generation, a royal priesthood, an holy nation, a peculiar people; that ye should shew forth the praises of him who hath called you out of darkness into his marvellous light;
¹⁰ Which in time past were not a people, but are now the people of God: which had not obtained mercy, but now have obtained mercy.

Ephesians 2:12-13
¹² That at that time ye were without Christ, being aliens from the commonwealth of Israel, and strangers from the covenants of promise, having no hope, and without God in the world:
¹³ But now in Christ Jesus ye who sometimes were far off are made nigh by the blood of Christ.

Ephesians 2:19-22
¹⁹ Now therefore ye are no more strangers and foreigners, but fellowcitizens with the saints, and of the household of God;
²⁰ And are built upon the foundation of the apostles and prophets, Jesus Christ himself being the chief corner stone;
²¹ In whom all the building fitly framed together groweth unto an holy temple in the Lord:
²² In whom ye also are builded together for an habitation of God through the Spirit.

Luke 17:21
²¹ *Neither shall they say, Lo here! or, lo there! for, behold, the kingdom of God is within you.*

HOUSE OF A KING

This lame man did not know that he was the house of the King of Kings and his body was the temple of the Holy Ghost. This lame man did not know that he was a son of Jesus. He did not know that he was the seed of Abraham by faith and the promise was by faith.

1 Corinthians 6:19
¹⁹ *What? know ye not that your body is the temple of the Holy Ghost which is in you, which ye have of God, and ye are not your own?*

John 14:2-3
² *In my Father's house are many mansions: if it were not so, I would have told you. I go to prepare a place for you.*
³ *And if I go and prepare a place for you, I will come again, and receive you unto myself; that where I am, there ye may be also.*

Biography Profile

Dr. S. Kiwi Kalloo was born in the Island of Trinidad. He came to know the Lord at the age of fifteen. Through the earnest yearning for the heart of God, led him down a very rough road but because his destiny was locked up in the face of Christ this was a road that he was sure to travel. He worked with believers in Christ Assembly from 1984 serving under Pastor Joseph Lamothe where he became seasoned in the Word of God and the things of God. The call of God upon his life led him to do a lot of things that brought him into a personal relationship with the Father. Being called of God in the office of a servant, he spent many days set-aside for his purpose. During this time he would go for days without food, water, or even contact with anyone.

His cravings for the Holy Spirit drove him into the wilderness, deep into the bushes, at the mountains of his hometown, a place called Corosal. He has experienced many visitations of God.

Under the leadership of Pastor Lamothe, Kiwi did the work of an evangelist. He laid hands on the sick and witnessed their recovery; prayed for those that were demon possessed and also saw their deliverance. He functioned as a worship leader, musician, and a minister from 1985 until now. He has supported numerous ministries and churches throughout the Trinidad. He ministered the Word in season and out of season. Kiwi has sought God's face, spending many late nights of study in the Word.

Kiwi is married to his beautiful wife, Lisa. They have three beautiful children Joanna, Justin and Jessica.

He was ordained as a Minister of the Gospel in 1991 and served under Pastor Joseph until he immigrated to the United States in 1995 where he submitted under the covering and leadership of Pastor Pepe when Miramar Christian Center (MCC) was in the process of being birthed. He was re-ordained as an associate Pastor with MCC in 1997.

He served under Pastor Pepe Ramnath as a Worship leader, an Associate Pastor, and a musician. He prophesied many events accurately as given unction by the Holy Spirit. He ministered in various churches in South Florida as a Minister of MCC and is still submitted under the covering of Pastor Pepe.

He migrated to New York City in 2001 and worked with several local churches. In 2012, Kiwi settled at Kingdom Life Ministries and accepted the call to be the Executive Pastor under the authority and leadership of Senior Pastor Dr. David C. Yankana.

Books by Dr. S. Kiwi Kalloo
The Baptism of Grace (The Blood Baptism)

Honors

Dr. S. Kiwi Kalloo has been recognized:

Anointed By God Chaplain
Dr. S. Kiwi Kalloo is certified by the Anointed by God Seminary as a Chaplain in conjunction with New York Regional Police; received an honorary doctorate from ABG as a Doctor of Divinity.

State of NY Chaplain
Certified by L.A.C.A.S.N.Y. as a Chaplain under the authority with New York State

Academy of Universal Global Peace
Received his Doctorate as Doctor of Philosophy from Academy of Universal Global Peace A.U.G.P. under his Excellency Dr. Madhu Krishan Chairman of A.U.G.P.
Holds the position as a Director and AMBASSADOR of PEACE under the authority of A.U.G.P. and its affiliates. Certified in many affiliate and Kingdom training programs.

Doctorate in (PhD)
    Establishing Peace Worldwide
    Literature
    Divinity
    Theology
    Biblical Studies
    Church Management and Organizational Administration
    Doctor of Ministry
    Church Music and Worship
    Leadership
    Educational Ministry
    Ambassador of Peace

Activities
    Author

Song Writer
Musician
Worship Leader
Leadership
Minister of the Word

Professional and Corporate

Dr. S. Kiwi Kalloo is the President and CEO of Kiwi Steel Corp, Located in South Ozone Park, NY.

Kiwi Steel Corp. is a structural and miscellaneous steel erector, certified as a Minority/Disadvantaged Business Enterprise in the New York and New Jersey.
Kiwi Steel Corp. has worked on several landmark projects:

> 911 Call Center located in Bronx, NY
> Police Academy located in College Point, NY
> Barclay's (Nets) Arena in Brooklyn, NY
> Terminal 4 Delta Facility at JFK Airport Terminal
> Columbia University-North Campus in Manhattanville, NY
> Columbia University MTA above ground train line, NY

He believes in strong leadership, perfection, cooperate anointing, present truth, divine order and maturity of the saints. His ministry is centered on the Heart of God in the Principles of the Kingdom in Sonship, Worship, and Maturity.

Contact Information

E-mail kiwi@kiwikalloo.com
Website www.kiwikalloo.com
Twitter: @KiwiKalloo
Facebook: www.facebook.com/kiwi.kalloo

Made in United States
Orlando, FL
30 October 2024